The Book That (Almost) Got Me Fired:

How I (Barely) Survived a Year in Corporate America

Kelly K. James

MSI Press, LLC

1760-F Airline Hwy #203

Hollister, CA 95023

Copyeditor: Betty Lou Leaver

Cover Design & Layout: Opeyemi Ikuborije

LCCN: 2023918199

ISBN: 978-1-957354-36-1

CONTENTS

To Ryan and Haley, who I love a tiny, tiny bit

Introduction

I'd had a reasonably successful career as a fulltime freelancer and ghostwriter when I decided to go "in-house" and take a fulltime job in January, 2019. I decided I'd take the job, and write about it, the way the late Barbara Ehrenreich did in *"Nickel and Dimed: On (Not) Getting By in America."* A year later, I had more than 130,000 words of notes, and spent the next couple of years writing the book you're holding in your hands (or more likely, perusing on an e-reader of some sort).

My goal was to write a prescriptive work memoir aimed at women who were reentering corporate America after years, or decades, away from it. I thought I'd be writing about how to work with people decades younger than myself, whether I could shoehorn my freelance mindset into a corporate structure, and whether a midlife woman could learn (lots of!) new skills and succeed in a completely new environment— and I did. But I also wound up writing about anxiety, single parenthood, female friendship, aging and body image, love, and gratitude.

In many cases, I've changed the names of the people who appear in this book; with others I've included their names, with their permission. I've told this story as truthfully as I can, and acknowledge that a memoir is by necessity drawn from a writer's memory and that the people who lived the story along with me may remember events differently.

My hope is that you'll enjoy the ride, and find the advice I share useful as you pursue your career goals, whatever they may be. Four and a half years after my first day at a company we'll call "Digital Edge," I'm still a fulltime wage worker (although at a different company) by day, and a freelance writer by night. I am grateful for the ability to write for a living, and to share my story with you.

Thank you for reading, and please reach out if you have questions about midlife career transitions, successful freelancing, the care and feeding of the creative mind, or you have great ideas for what I can make for dinner tonight.

CHAPTER 1

Candidacy

"So, why would you apply for this position?" Frank Becker, manager of the content department at Digital Edge, leaned back in his chair, his arms folded across his chest.

It was a reasonable question. After all, I'd been freelancing full-time for nearly 22 years. Now I was interviewing for a job. A full-time job. A (gasp) real job.

I'd applied for the content specialist position on a whim. Digital Edge was three miles from my home, and the brief job description sounded like work I could do. I submitted a resume and a cover letter the day before Thanksgiving and had already forgotten about it when I received an email the Monday after the holiday to schedule an interview.

I hadn't expected a reply, must less an interview, so I did a little quick research before I drove over to meet with Frank. Per its website, Digital Edge specialized in internet marketing, including SEO and PPC campaigns. I'd written SEO (Search Engine Optimization) content for freelance clients in the past but had no clue what PPC was until I Googled it a half-hour before the interview. PPC stood for Pay Per Click, as in online advertising.

"I'm going to be completely transparent," I told Frank. He was about my age, stocky, with a closely cropped haircut. He wore a pullover sweater and jeans while I was sporting one of my favorite grown-up outfits—a black, white, and blue patterned skirt with a black scoop-necked blouse.

"I got divorced two-and-a-half years ago. The first year, you're just kind of scrambling, trying to manage all the changes, make sure your kids are okay, keep it together, and try not to cry at random moments," I said. "The second year is more like, 'okay, this is what life looks like now,' things are settling down, you're not completely freaked out anymore, you've got some mental space to handle stuff. The third year is like, 'okay, what does the rest of my life look like? What do I do now?'"

Frank nodded, probably wondering how much more of my personal life I was going to offer up during the rest of our interview. (Spoiler alert: pretty much all of it.)

"Well, that's where I'm at now. And let me just say—health insurance is a driver for me. The cost is killing me," I said, ignoring the irony. "The other thing is, I love what I do as a ghostwriter. I have a really close relationship with a client for six, nine, twelve months while I'm writing the person's book. Then, the book is done, and, bam! I'm on to the next client and the next project. That can get old.

"I'm an extrovert in an introvert's job," I explained to Frank. I told him that every morning after dropping my daughter off at school, I drove to the Peet's coffeehouse about a mile from my house. I ordered a large skim latte, minus a shot, and sat at the end of the long cedar table in the corner, eavesdropping on conversations and taking breaks to chat with my compatriots who followed a similar routine. There were Chuck and Bill, both of whom were in insurance. Sy, a financial advisor. My friend Mary, a retired social worker. Jordan, a 20-something who worked with special needs kids and was writing a young adult novel between appointments. Roger, one of the founders of Spenga. My neighbor Kevin, a retired broker who was learning Spanish for fun. I spent the mornings at Peet's, banging out articles and books, drove home for lunch, and spent the rest of the day with my feet propped up, working from a corner of the couch in my living room, which I called Command Central. Then, my kids came home from school, and I parented the rest of the day.

Frank asked about some of my freelance experience, and as we talked, I wondered if I should admit that I'd applied for the job on a whim. While I was finishing my best year money-wise in more than a decade, I was feeling more and more anxious about continuing to freelance. Most of my income stemmed from writing books and book proposals for clients, but the work could be erratic. Sometimes, projects got tied up for weeks at a time, languishing on an agent's or editor's desk.

I liked to work, and I liked to work hard. I didn't mind banging out 10-hour days or working nights and weekends if necessary to meet a client's deadline. What I did mind was having to deal with dead days where I didn't have work. An occasional day with little to do let me reboot. Consecutive days left me feeling uneasy, underutilized, and scared. As a ghostwriter, I was always looking for my next project, and those projects weren't always coming at the speed I needed to maintain both consistent cash flow and work.

A year before, in a fit of money-driven anxiety, I'd applied to a slew of full-time jobs, with the single-minded intent of securing health insurance. When I was married, health insurance wasn't on my financial radar. When I got divorced, my former husband, Erik, and I agreed to keep the kids on his health insurance, but I saw the monthly premium for mine climb to $600 a month—for a $5,000 deductible policy which didn't even cover the cost of the selective serotonin reuptake inhibitor I took for anxiety, which was both effective and expensive at $330/month. Add in the cost of my shrink,

Molly, whom I saw every month or so, and I was spending nearly $10,000 a year on my health care.

And I was healthy, except for my lifelong companion of anxiety which flared up now and then, chronic insomnia, and ongoing issues with my left knee and right hip, both of which were no doubt aggravated by my insistence on continuing to run nearly every morning in an ongoing attempt to manage my anxiety. While my 52-year-old body was starting to complain, a hard session on the treadmill was the most effective way of burning off the swirling mist of existential angst I woke to nearly every morning.

None of the jobs I'd applied for had panned out, so I'd recommitted to marketing myself and rebuilding (yet again) my freelance business. I'd been doing this for more than 20 years, and in the past, I'd always been able to shake fruit (or in this case, clients and work) loose from the trees and wind up with enough work and enough money.

While I got a little maintenance and child support from my former husband, Erik, the last couple of years I'd been making barely enough to support myself, my 13-year-old son and nearly-9-year-old daughter. Earlier that year I'd had several promising book projects fall through, and while I was working on a couple of proposals for ghosting clients, there was no guarantee that they would sell. No sale meant no book, which meant no work, no money, and even more anxiety.

I didn't share all of that with Frank, but I was candid about the fact that I had two school-aged kids. That I was 52. That after a less-than-satisfying career as a lawyer, I had been self-employed for more than 20 years. "Honestly, the idea of taking a full-time job is kind of scary. I don't know that I can give up the freedom and flexibility I have. Also," I added, "I'm pretty sure I've covered everything you can't legally ask me in this interview." I laughed.

Frank nodded and steered the conversation away from my random inappropriate disclosures and explained what the position would entail. The content strategist job was a newly created position, the first of its kind.

As the content strategist, I would be the liaison between the SEO and content departments. Digital Edge worked with mostly small and medium-sized businesses doing internet marketing campaigns designed to increase the number of "qualified leads" (potential customers) that websites brought in. The SEO team did research to determine what search terms, or keywords, a client's page should contain. Keywords were the phrases that potential customers used when looking for that type of business.

"I need a businessperson who thinks like a writer," he said. "Or a writer who thinks like a businessperson."

That was me. I'd built my career on the idea that I was a businessperson first and writer second and had developed a niche as a successful freelancer, even writing books about how others could do the same. "I can do that," I said aloud. "I *do* do that." I looked at him. "It does sound interesting. It's more a conceptualizing/big picture type of job than a writing job. Correct?"

He nodded. "But there would likely be some writing involved."

"I'd like that. I have done a fair amount of writing for the web," I said, though most of my background was in the dying medium of print. I looked at the outline samples. "How many of these would I be expected to produce in a day?"

He held up his hands. "I can't answer that. Because this is a new position, we're not sure yet what it will look like. We've had people in Atlanta—we have another office there—creating outlines but we need someone here who can take them over as we migrate clients to our Digital Plus model. The content specialist will be responsible for those clients."

The job sounded intriguing. I'd already confirmed that the company offered health insurance to its full-time employees. And the chair I was sitting in was quite comfortable. "Wow! I have to say, it sounds like a great fit for me! Give me $80,000, and I'm yours!" So much for any kind of thoughtful salary negotiation! The number fell out of my mouth without thinking about it.

Frank uncrossed his arms and leaned forward in his chair. "This position is considered entry-level," he warned, looking down at his notes. "The salary associated with the position is $35,000."

$35,000? A year? I was at the stage of my ghostwriting career where I made around $40,000 for a book, typically writing a book a year along with other work like book proposals and articles that got my income up to the $60,000 or $70,000 range, hopefully even more. Now I was single and didn't have the luxury of a second (not to mention much larger) paycheck, I needed to make that much.

"Oh." I sat back. "I can't do that."

Frank didn't argue. "There is another position here that we're hiring for," said Frank, passing me another job description. "It's a position for editor." That job paid $45,000, which was still low.

I glanced at it and shook my head. "Editing isn't my strong suit," I said. "I'd get bored doing nothing but editing all day." I liked to research, to write, to create frameworks for articles and books and then fill them in. While I had edited a couple of books for clients, I'd only done developmental or "big picture" editing, not line editing where you checked grammar, spelling and punctuation, following a style guide like *The Chicago Manual of Style* or *The Associated Press Stylebook*. I knew they had differences but had never bothered to figure out what they were. When an editor said something like, "We use AP," I'd think, "Cool!" and leave it at that, assuming that it was the editor's job to make sure that the stylebook was being followed.

Frank seemed to sense that any interest I had in the job was evaporating. "I think you'd be a great fit for this position," said Frank. "I'm willing to go to the partners here to see if I can authorize a higher salary, if you're interested."

"I appreciate that," I said. "But honestly, I've been freelancing for so long I don't know if I can sit in an office all day." Once again, I spoke without considering the impact my words might have.

"Why not give it a try? Give it six months. It doesn't work out, you go back to freelancing. Hell, give it two months. I think you could do a lot for the company in this role. You could take the position and run with it."

Gosh! When was the last time a client had gunned for me like that? I was always the one chasing down clients and nailing down work.

"Let me give you a tour of the office," Frank said. We'd been sitting in the CEO's office—the partners had their own offices while the rest of the staff worked in one large room, sitting at mini cubicle farms of six desks each. The room was large, with high ceilings and glass windows on all sides. It was well-lit and relatively quiet, considering there were about 50 people throughout the room. Most were in their 20s, with a few more seasoned employees scattered throughout. The majority were men, and at least half wore headphones, which explained the lack of conversation. Nearly everyone was dressed in sweatshirts and jeans. I knew the office had a casual dress code, but this had the feel of a college library more than a workplace.

Most of the employees' eyes were glued to their giant screens, but several glanced up and smiled at me as I walked by with Frank. ("They thought it was bring-your-grandma-to-work day," said my neighbor Brian later.) The vibe seemed … good. Comfortable. No one appeared to be actively miserable, at least as far as I could see.

I met Roger, the other man I'd be working with closely. Like Frank, he was a former sports reporter and editor, a few years older than I, and had an easygoing, rumpled look about him. I saw several younger guys in their late 20s or early 30s pacing near the back of the building. They were good-looking, fit guys with cordless headsets, and I could tell from the brief snatches of conversation that they were in sales.

Frank showed me the "nook," a little kitchen stocked with coffee, bagels, and bowl full of carb-heavy packaged snacks, the meeting rooms, and the cafeteria. Then. he asked if I had any other questions and asked me to get back in touch with him if I did.

I couldn't take the job at $35,000. Before- and after-school childcare for Haley would push my salary into the minimum wage zone. But what if the company offered me more? A lot more? Was it willing to give it a try, as Frank had suggested? Why not? It could be an adventure.

"I think I want this job," I said as I walked down the stairs of the building. By the time I climbed into "Cherry Cherry," the bright red 2018 HRV I was leasing. a few seconds later, the feeling had crystalized.

"Holy shit," I said aloud. "I do want this job."

I met my friend, Chris, a fellow freelancer who worked as a marketing consultant, for lunch immediately after my interview. "I think I'm going to take it," I said. "What do you think?"

"You can't not take it! It's health insurance. It's three miles from your house. And for some reason, they actually want you!" He took a giant bite of his pulled pork sandwich.

"But I can't do it for $35,000, so I have to see what the offer is," I countered. "The health insurance is great. But I'm going to have to pay for childcare again, and I haven't had to do that since Haley started school. I think I'm worth at least $80,000, but the company seems to be pretty cheap in terms of salary, so I think my number is going to be $60,000. Maybe $50,000." After all, health insurance would save me at least $10,000 and that was after-tax money.

Chris nodded. "That sounds fair."

"You know, the fact that they're even willing to take a chance on someone who's been self-employed for most of her career is significant," I said. "Besides, if it's horrible, I can always quit."

"Oh, that's a great attitude," said Chris. "If you wind up taking it, take it with the intention of succeeding at it. Give yourself six months—or a year—before you decide whether it's working for you." He took another bite of his sandwich. "You should commit to it for a year," he said, his mouth full.

The next morning, I listed the potential pros and cons of the job. I'd done this for years whenever I felt my enthusiasm for freelancing flagging. Enumerating the pros (I'm in charge of my own career; I can make my own schedule; I like the work I do; I'm making $40,000/book) had always managed to let me downplay the cons (super-expensive yet crappy health insurance; little security; the constant need to market myself; the feast-or-famine nature of the work).

Pros of Taking the Job

1. I'd have health insurance. For a lot less than what I was paying now. It meant I could finally get that colonoscopy I'd had my eye on! At nearly 53, I knew I couldn't put it off forever.

2. It was convenient. The office was 3.2 miles from my house, per my Maps app. It would take maybe 15 minutes to get there—assuming I didn't encounter a train on the way to work. (My town is bisected by train tracks, and you can easily get hung up for 10 or 15 minutes if a couple of freight trains roll through.)

3. The company wanted me. Visions of Sally Field— "You like me! You really like me!"—notwithstanding, it was flattering to be wanted. Frank had said he knew I could do the job. He'd said he'd go to the partners to get more money for me. He wanted me! And I loved to be wanted.

4. I'd know how much money I would make. Twice a month, every month, money would be deposited into my bank account. Every month. I would no longer worry (okay, obsess) over whether, or when, I'd be paid.

5. I could continue to freelance. This was key. I had a couple of clients that I wanted to retain, including Nancy, an Instagram influencer who wrote about how to eat to "heal and seal" your gut if you had digestive issues like irritable bowel syndrome. I'd worked on her proposal for the last seven months, rewriting it three times, and her agent was finally about to shop it around. I wanted to write the book itself if it sold.

Cons of Taking the Job

1. I'd have to actually, you know, show up to work. Every day. With actual clothes on. My kids, neighbors, and most people who know me are aware of my penchant for outfits built around overalls and Birkenstocks, a fact that caused my 9-year-old-fashionista-in-the-making daughter some anguish. I knew that more would be expected, even required, with even a "casual" dress code.

2. I'd be sitting. All day. At a desk. As a writer, I sat a lot, but I broke up that time. I worked at Peet's in the morning, went home for lunch, and broke up my afternoon with walks around the block and trips to the basement to throw in a load of wash or quick trips to the grocery store. Almost every Friday, I took a long, lazy lunch and often took the rest of the afternoon off.

3. I'd be saying good-bye to my freedom. See number two. Freelancing = freedom. The words even start with the same syllable! I would have to answer to a boss, account for my time, deal with coworkers, meetings, office politics, and all of the other corporate headaches that the regularly employed simply accepted as the norm. The thought made me a bit stabby.

4. The what ifs. What if I simply couldn't do the work? What if some of the people I worked with didn't like me? What if none of them liked me? What if they nicknamed me Granny, made comments about needing a walker, or otherwise let me know that I was … old? After all, 52 seemed ancient when I was in my 20s. (Forget "50 is the new 30." We all know this is bullshit we Gen Xers try to sell to each other on the

regular, but the fact is that at 50, you're looking at the second half of your life, not the first.) What if they all went out for drinks and didn't invite me? What if they did invite me, and I could think of nothing to say? Who would I talk to in the lunchroom? I'd forgotten most of what I once knew about working in an office environment, and I knew next to nothing about Millennials other than that they were the most-maligned generation.

5. I was giving up, wasn't I? I'd been a fairly successful freelancer for more than 20 years. I'd written books on successful freelancing, had written dozens of columns and articles on the subject, and spoken at more than 50 writers' conferences. I had developed a niche in freelancing expertise, and even when I'd segued into ghostwriting, I'd kept that identity alive. In considering a job, with a boss, with a workplace, with benefits, wasn't I admitting, "I can't hack it?" I'd pushed through slow periods before, but I'd never come close to even considering caving and getting a full-time job. And if I wasn't a freelancer anymore, then who would I be? I'd been a freelancer longer than I'd been a wife. Longer than I'd been a mom. My freelancing time had easily comprised the bulk of my adulthood and my career. If I said, "so long," what did that say about me?

When I looked at the list, I realized I'd forgotten the fact that a job meant that I would have a place to go, 8.5 hours a day. I'd thought that might be a con, but my anxiety had been ratcheting up over the last few months. Like the slow tick/tick/tick of a wooden rollercoaster on its ascent, I could feel it creeping up on me. I ran more, consciously worked on deep breathing, stopped trying to multitask (so much), and talked to my shrink. Yet, it was growing, incrementally, but inevitably, and I was running out of tools to manage it.

Being in a place where I was given work to do, and doing it, would provide a certain amount of consistency. Of routine. Of enough demands that I would return home pleasantly but not exhaustively tired. I'd have punched my work ticket for the day, and my evenings would be spent parenting consciously, intelligently, and thoughtfully. (Was I rose-colored-glassing my future? Of course. But I was too enamored of the idea that my anxiety might be under control to give it much mind.)

I was so enamored that I capitulated on the salary. My plan was to hold out for $50,000, but the partners held firm at $45,000. Frank was apologetic but made it clear that the figure had no flexibility. It was a take-or-leave-it situation.

My gut had told me I wanted the job. But the what-ifs threatened to swamp me before I accepted it. I called my longtime friend Polly, a fellow freelancer who wrote extensively about spirituality while being one of my few friends who swore nearly as much as I did.

"I'm taking it," I said, a little breathlessly. I was walking to the store a half-mile from my house to pick up cat food and get a quick exercise break in the middle of the day. "And I'm going to write about it. I'm going to write about my experience," I said, warming to the idea. "I've already got 2,200 words written, and I don't start for three weeks!"

"Hell, you can write the book before you even start the job!" she yelled. "Just leave a bunch of blanks to fill in, and then tell people they have to do stuff so you can finish the book." We cackled.

I told her I'd be working with a lot of Millennials. "I know next to nothing about Millennials," I said. "Hashtag clueless. Except I know hashtag is outdated too."

"Shit! I just started saying hashtag!" We cackled some more. "Well, I'm 50, and I don't give a shit anymore. The other day I said something apparently sarcastic and; Jerry said, 'that was unnecessary,' and I said, 'who cares?'"

Because that's what happens around the time you hit 50. You no longer give a shit what people think. Polly and I gabbed and cackled and swore some more. Before she hung up, she offered some advice.

"You said you've anxious about the job," she said. "Of course, you're anxious. You've been freelancing for like 20 fucking years!"

"Twenty-two," I interrupted.

"Whatever. Anything new is going to make anyone anxious. Especially a smart person. But you'll get into it. You'll freak out sometimes, and it will be fine. You got this."

"Yeah, I do."

"And write! Write it all down! I gotta know what corporate America looks like nowadays."

"I will." I hung up and tossed cans of cat food into my canvas tote, thinking about what she'd said. Yes, new things are bound to make you anxious. That was normal, not diagnosable. Instead of fretting over my anxiety, I could treat it as excitement, the natural response to something novel or new. Wow. That seemed a lot more palatable.

A few days before my first day at work, I ran into Sy, a 50-something financial planner whom I knew from Peet's. "I heard you took a job!" he said, and I filled him in on what I'd seen and what I expected.

"You don't know what it will be like until you get in there," he said. "It's like dating. Someone sounds amazing on paper, then you start going out, and two weeks later, you're like what the hell was I thinking?" He drank some coffee. "You know, I quit a job after three days once. I was hired to be the CFO

16

for a carpet company. It was a family-owned business, and during the three days, not one person came into my office to introduce themselves. So, I quit. You get in there; it turns out to be not what you expected, and you quit —well, you haven't risked anything. You can still go back to freelancing and ramp up your book business."

I nodded, trying to keep up with him.

"So, it's a Millennial work environment?" Sy continued. "I've never worked in a Millennial environment. I mean, I know Millennials, but I haven't worked with them. I usually run from them."

I laughed. "Well, I know a few Millennials," I countered, thinking of Mel, who bartended at the pool hall where I played in a weekly league. And Jordan from Peet's. I know two Millennials, I thought proudly. And I like them. And they like me! That had to bode well for my future employment.

But even if I could connect with my Millennial coworkers (I hoped), I wasn't in my 20s anymore. Or my 30s. Or even my 40s. Most days, that didn't bother me. Others, I was simultaneously amazed and horrified that I'd gotten so old. I consoled myself with the fact I looked okay, even pretty damn good some days, with clothes on, and I wasn't in a profession like pole dancing where the perceived perfection of my body truly mattered.

Even so, a harsh or unflattering light revealed a whole host of indignities. Sun damage. Sagging skin. Cherry angiomas splattered across my torso. Cellulite on body parts that had never before had cellulite—like the fronts of my upper arms. When had that happened? Random body hairs that had never appeared before—like a chin hair as coarse as toothbrush bristle that would sprout appear every few weeks. In addition to my forehead lines, I was now sporting two vertical lines between my eyebrows that were apparently permanent. Recently, I'd developed the dreaded "meno-pot" and was starting to understand why women of a certain age opted for flowing tunic tops and loose waistlines.

But I was healthy, I reminded myself. And strong. My body, apart from various running maladies that cropped up now and again, could still hammer out four miles on the treadmill in a little over 36 minutes. I lifted weights a couple of times a week. I could (and did) shovel my driveway every time it snowed.

Most days I felt pretty good when I woke up. About 25. And since I'd been feeling 25 since I was actually 25, I was hopeful that I could keep my youthful outlook permanently.

Still, some things had changed. While I'd had student loans and the stress of a career as a newbie attorney to contend with, those worries were small fry compared to being a parent. My biggest ones almost always revolved around my kids and tended to center on whether I was doing a decent job as a parent or failing spectacularly.

In theory, the idea of freelancing and parenting full time worked. I had flexibility and adapted my schedule to the kids'. But the reality was that as a single mom, I was often distracted, stressed out, tired, or simply crabby with my kids. Then, I felt guilty about being a horrible parent. Even when I felt that I was doing okay, I was always peripherally aware of how fast my parenting time was elapsing. But was I truly enjoying it? Was I doing the best I could? Most days I simply was grateful to have two healthy, (mostly) happy, well-adjusted children whose biggest problems were that they weren't allowed to have an Xbox and television in his room (Ryan) and were forbidden to sit on my iPhone all day, making Tik Tok videos (Haley).

I was balancing my desire to be a good (well, great) mom with my desire to have a man in my life again. My boyfriend, Walt, didn't have kids and had never dated anyone with them.

He had soon discovered that I oriented my entire life around my kids, as parents do.

Since we lived an hour apart (we met online, thanks to Zoosk), we typically only saw each on weekends. The kids were with me for ten days and with Erik for four, and on those weekends, I was free … unless Ryan had a travel basketball tournament or Haley had a soccer game or some other event that I didn't want to miss. On the weekends the kids were with me, Walt was thrown into an insta-family whether he wanted one or not. I wasn't sure whether he did, which meant I wasn't sure whether we had a future together though we'd been going out for nearly a year.

On paper, we were a mismatch. I tended to rush and juggle and multitask and to always be thinking of the next thing. He was a union plumber who walked slowly, talked slowly, and moved slowly. He was thoughtful, measured, and calm. While I was always striving for the next project, the next client, or the next challenge, his default was set at "content." I was maddened by it even while I envied his ease in the world, with himself, with everyone.

I'd been attracted to that ease and loved that he made me laugh, that he rarely lost his temper, and that he called me Zippy. I loved his size, his smile, his big rough hands that were always scratched and scarred, and the way he always looked out for me. He was constantly fixing stuff in my house that I didn't realize needed fixing. Hell, he unclogged my shower drain on our second date! For Mother's Day, he bought me a toilet, replaced the old one in my basement bathroom, and helped me clean out and organize my garage, which I hadn't done since moving in more than two years prior.

But he didn't read books, and he wasn't interested in architecture, museums, or foreign films. He watched terrible network TV … what I considered pablum for the masses, like

America's Got Talent or *The Masked Singer* or whatever idiotic show was broadcast on a typical weekday night. He didn't even have cable! He didn't bring much to the intellectual party that I often wanted to host—not like most of my friends, whom I tended to cherry-pick for being well-read, intelligent, and insightful. Because at heart, I'm an intellectual snob.

Dating Walt was like tending a hard-to-kill houseplant. I didn't have to put in much time or energy into our relationship because we didn't see other that often. The relationship thrived even with minimal care. And minimal care was what I needed. I'd spent a lot of time and emotional energy putting my toe back into the dating pool and had had more than a dozen in-person "encounters" (I refused to call them dates) with men I'd met online, looking for someone I had a connection with. That had proved to be more difficult than I'd expected.

Since my divorce, I'd only met two men I was attracted to, and the fact was I'd known both of them beforehand. Gabriel and I had been members of the local swimming pool board together, and after his divorce, he'd bought a house down the street from me. We'd gotten to know each other better after he moved in, and I'd found that I liked him. A lot. He was smart, well-read, funny, and sexy, and also very freshly divorced. Two of his kids had been adopted, and we talked about everything from adoption to marriage to sex to heartbreak to the meaning of life and our favorite standup comedians. Gabriel got my literary references and obscure jokes and deftly returned my conversational volleys. We bantered back and forth by phone or text and called each other "twin" for thinking the same thing so often.

But Gabriel was still grieving the loss of his marriage and family and trying to figure out what his life was going to look like. I didn't want to get involved with him and have my heart broken and knew we were better off as friends.

"You need pussy," I'd told him. "You need transition pussy, and I am not going to be your transition pussy." He'd burst out laughing and agreed, and we'd settled into a friendship unlike one I'd had before. We flirted. Joked, and tried to impress each other with our big words, secure in the knowledge that we weren't going to have a Relationship. Or even sex. We'd discovered our former marriages had had a lot in common and worked on what I called bucket-filling.

"Have I told you how smart you are? Super smart. And you're a good dad, a good son, and a good brother; you can fix anything, and you are incredibly handsome," I'd tell him. "You know that, right?"

"Gee, thanks," Gabriel would say, laughing.

"Seriously," I'd continue. "You are the complete package. Any woman would be so lucky to be with you. All my friends say the same thing."

"You're filling my bucket again, right?"

"Well, yeah," I'd say. "But I mean it."

While I was getting to know Gabriel, I'd started dating the only other available man in Downers Grove I found attractive, a widower with three kids who lived around the corner from me. He and I worked out at the Y in the mornings. I had been attracted to Richard's confidence and had flirted with him rather brazenly until he'd asked me out.

Richard made me nervous. He was cocky, funny, and sexy, and he made me feel desirable for the first time in literally years. He also had some anger issues which often bubbled to the surface, but I'd fallen into bed with him, anyway. I'd been reminded of how much I'd missed having sex. The more sex we had, the better it got. Soon, I was thinking there was something between us, when what we actually had was a no-strings sexual relationship that worked for him because I was convenient. Even so, I wound up "catching feelings" and was stung when he dumped me. By text. (Something I likely had in common with plenty of Millennials.)

Months later, I was still smarting when I'd met Walt. I'd even warned him about it the first night we met. Walt hadn't blinked. He'd made me laugh, listened to the torrent of information I needed to offload, and even survived what I thought was a subtle grilling designed to reveal his political beliefs and any possible racist or homophobic tendencies. He'd not only passed but surprised me over the months with his ability to remember even minor details of my life I'd mentioned in one of our less-than-fascinating phone calls.

Whatever might happen, for now Walt and I were solid. My kids were doing well. I was taking a job. What did that mean for my freelance career? I talked to my agent, Katherine, about my upcoming transition and my plan to jettison a book client who'd been dragging his feet on a proposal but to keep Nancy's book. She understood my reasoning and supported my decision but cautioned me against disclosing my new employee status on Facebook or LinkedIn.

"I know you can work full time and ghostwrite on the side, but you don't want it to appear that you're doing anything that could be perceived as violating your contracts," she explained. She was right. Every book contract included a provision prohibiting me from taking on any other project that might interfere with my ability to complete the book.

Shit, I hadn't thought this all the way through. I had already determined that I didn't want to completely burn my freelance bridges—what if the job didn't work out? What if I started and it turned out I hated it? What if I got fired just a few days or weeks in? Then, I'd be really screwed. Keeping my book project and a few other freelance clients was my idea of a safety net and one I wasn't willing to jump without. I promised

Katherine I'd keep my employee status strictly private, at least for a while.

The Corporate Newbie's Cheat Sheet: Should You Take the Job?

You've been offered the job. Congrats! But hold on a minute. Do you want the job? Really want it? You're facing a big decision here.

First, do your due diligence. Have you obtained as much information as you can about the job? What will your responsibilities entail? Will you be working on site, remotely, or a combination of both? What's the salary? What benefits will you receive? How much will benefits (like health insurance!) cost you? How long will your commute be if you have to go to the office?

I suggest you make two lists: one of the possible pros of taking the job and another of the possible drawbacks. Compare the two.

Finally, picture what your life will look like if you take the job. Will you need childcare? A dog walker? A new wardrobe or at least a few new outfits? If you're changing jobs, will you be working more hours or fewer than before? Will your day-to-day schedule change radically (like if you haven't been working and are going in-house) or look similar to what it is now?

Ask yourself one final question: how do you feel about taking the job? Excited? Happy? A little nervous? All are good. A lack of excitement or the sense that you're settling because you're desperate, not so much. Ideally, you're taking a job that offers a new opportunity, reasonable pay, and an environment you think you can thrive in for the coming months or years. If that feels like the case, accept that job, and uncork the Champagne!

CHAPTER 2

Onboarding

The night before I started the job, I couldn't sleep. I passed out sometime around midnight, woke up about 4:00 a.m., and caught snatches of stress-dream-laden sleep before I finally dragged myself out of bed a little before 6:00 a.m.

I followed my regular routine. I peed, drank a big glass of water (always on a quest to achieve optimal hydration), fed the cat, and cracked open a Diet Mountain Dew. I checked my email, dressed in workout gear, and forced myself to the gym where I banged out four miles on the treadmill, a punishing run that smoothed the sharpest of the knife edges off of my anxiety.

After I showered, I did my hair, applied makeup, and slid into my version of grown-up clothes (a gray-and-black patterned blouse, my favorite black skirt, black tights, and black platform shoes), made a sandwich, and checked on the kids, who were both still asleep, thanks to winter break. Ryan would be in charge of his sister for the day.

My commute took 17 minutes, consistent with the test run I'd done the week before. I called Frank from the foyer, and he met me at the door, ushering me into the office, and walked me to my cubicle, diagonally from his and three seats away from the window. I smiled and waved at Roger, met Evie, the editor, who sat behind me, and Daniel, a good-looking 20-something sales guy, who sat to my right.

My name and "Content Specialist" hung on a plastic placard in the corner of my cube, slightly askew. I tried not to take that as a bad omen. A Digital Edge T-shirt, coffee mug, and backpack sat in a neat pile under a sticky note that read, "WELCOME, KELLY!" I went to log onto my Mac only to discover that I had left my datebook, with my Digital Edge password written neatly on the inside cover, at home. I called and woke up Haley, who located it, and I logged on to my work computer for the first time ever.

I already had email! Most were from Frank, about how to request time off in the company's HR software and notes about Digital Edge style preferences. He and I met in Yahoo, one of the company's three conference rooms and the only one without windows. "You know, this used to be the room we used to fire employees," Frank said in passing.

What to say to that? "Okay?" I managed.

Frank then ticked the list on his mini legal pad, listing what was expected of me. I was to be on time every morning. If for some reason I was going to be late, I was to text him and let him know. I could keep my phone out on my desk, but it had to be on mute. If I took a call, I was to step out into the hallway outside the main office or the "cafeteria," which was just a large room with microwaves, a large refrigerator and several long tables with chairs. "I realize that we all have our phones nearby at all times," he said. "I realize you're going to be texting, but be mindful of how you do that. I had one guy who had his feet up and was texting on his phone when one of the partners walked by. That's not a good look for my team."

Frank continued along these kinds of expectations. "Your shift is 8:00 to 4:30, with half an hour for lunch," he said. "And 8:00 means you should be at your desk at 8:00 and ready to work, not coming at 8:00 and then grabbing coffee and getting set up." He continued in this vein while I listened and nodded.

After a few minutes, though, I held up my hand. "I understand all of this," I said. "I realize that you work with Millennials and maybe you have to tell them all this. But you don't have to tell me. I'm a grown-up." In grown-up clothes, I almost added.

Frank shook his head. "It's not just Millennials that I have to have this conversation with. I've had 40-year-olds who couldn't show up for work on time," he said. "One guy was late four out of five mornings his first week."

"You're kidding."

"Not at all. He blamed the traffic coming out from the city—well, you knew where you lived when you took this job."

"I can't imagine," I said. And I couldn't. Who was late to work the first week of a new job? After I spoke with Frank, I met with Sean, a bearded guy in his mid-30s who was wearing a T-shirt and jeans like most of his coworkers. Sean used the screen in the Google conference room to demonstrate the company's CMS, or Content Management System. I'd never had to use a CMS before, but it seemed to function like Facebook—people sent you messages through it, "tagging" you to notify you of tasks—but I came out of the meeting without a complete understanding of how to use it. I could figure that out on my own.

After my meeting with Sean, Frank walked me through the office to meet the various employees. He said a lot of names, and I shook a lot of hands. Mostly with Millennials. Mostly dudes. Some stood up when they met me (good job, Moms!). Some barely made eye contact. All shook my hand, but some had sweaty palms or weak, soft grips (I squashed the urge to correct them on the spot). Men outnumbered women about three to one, and the average age appeared to be mid

20s, though I met a few who were clearly in their 30s or older. The overriding work look was jeans paired with a sweatshirt or T-shirt, and I realized I was overdressed.

When I returned to my desk, I had a few more emails, along with a list from Frank of clients I was responsible for creating outlines for. I started plowing through the list, reviewing client websites, absorbing information, and trying not to think unproductive thoughts like, "How many more years can I do this?" and "Have I made a terrible mistake?"

But no signs pointed to the latter. I read up on the dozens of clients I'd be working on, and I could feel my anxious brain start to fire and absorb and plot. I'd be writing about ball bearings. Flower essences. High-end trips to Antarctica to see the Northern Lights. Custom athletic socks. Criminal law. Dentistry. Property management.

I settled into my comfortable chair and chose a client to start with. The company sold and repaired compressed air systems. I was to create the outline for a landing page (a page that a company's home page links to and one that is visible to Google) that highlighted the fact that our client serves clients in the oil and gas industry and included the relevant keywords. This, I'd discover later, was a common SEO tactic—create a "hub page" for industries or specialties or locations, and then list the relevant industries or specialties or locations below it, creating landing pages for each.

The keywords for this particular page were: oil and gas compressed air services, oil and gas compressed air management, oil and gas compressed air system engineering, oil and gas compressed air automation, oil and gas compressed air system audit, oil and gas compressed air systems design. Keywords, I knew from earlier experience with SEO, were the phrases that potential customers might type in when looking for a company to, in this case, meet their oil and gas compressed air services needs.

After reading through the client's website, I Googled phrases like "how is compressed air used in the oil and gas industry" and found some background that gave me a jumping-off point. I then created a brief outline, asking that the writer "create a new web page explaining that ABC Company serves clients in the oil and gas industry. Describe why/how compressed air systems are used in the oil and gas industry and the benefits of compressed air systems from ABC Company," and included some links as resources for the writer. Then, I wrote several more outlines for pages for different industries like agriculture, energy, and food and beverage. I still wasn't quite certain about how compressed air was used in these industries, but I didn't have to be. It would be the writer's job to figure it out.

The next client was B2C, or business to consumer, not business to business (B2B), and was easier to tackle. The company sold one product, a "cooler rest"—a metal backrest that hooked on to a full-size cooler, turning the cooler into a more comfortable seat. The client's homepage was thin on content, with only about 50 words. To please Google, the page would need at least 450 words of crawlable content, so the existing content would have to be expanded.

I'd done enough copywriting to know the difference between features (attributes of a product or service) and benefits, the reasons why someone might opt to purchase it. Both were essential for compelling copy, as was a CTA, or call to action, that spurred a customer to make a purchase. I created several more outlines for additional pages aimed at hunters, tailgaters, and boaters.

While the features and benefits of the product remained the same, the challenge for the writer would be to take that info and tweak it for difference audiences. I'd done this for years as a freelancer, writing about the same subject from different angles for different markets. This kind of "reslanting" let me maximize my research time and helped boost my income as well.

The next client was a retailer of ball bearings. We were adding product category pages, highlighting the different types of ball bearings the company sold; this particular site was an e-com, or e-commerce site, which meant you could buy directly through the site itself. With zero knowledge about ball bearings, I started with background reporting and wound up on Wikipedia. I'd soon spend more time on Wiki getting up to speed on previously-unknown-to-me subjects and industries than I could have imagined.

I'd not known that there were a slew of different types of bearings. Spherical bearings, Angular contact bearings. Ball and roller bearings. Mounted unit bearings. The first outline was for a page for spherical roller bearings with keywords: spherical roller bearings, spherical roller bearing types, double row spherical roller bearing, spherical roller thrust bearing, self- aligning spherical roller bearing, axial spherical roller bearing.

Now, I had questions. Some of the keywords were singular, not plural. Did that matter? Could I add an "s" to a keyword? Could self-aligning have a hyphen, or was I supposed to leave it out for Google? I didn't know, and I didn't want to admit that I didn't know as I had implied in my interview that I knew more about SEO than I in fact did. Quite a bit more.

I posed the question to Frank, who told me about "stop words," or words that Google didn't "count." That meant if your keyword was "plumber Naperville," you could write "plumber in Naperville," "plumber near Naperville," or "plumber for Naperville." As for whether I could make a word plural? "That's a question for SEO," he said, indicating the group of guys who sat on the opposite of the room.

Yes, but who from SEO? I looked at my seating chart, trying to determine whom I should ask. I decided on Seth, who sat by in the same six-pack as Sean. Seth told me that typically the search volume was the same for a term whether it was singular or plural, and that a hyphen operated like a stop word, meaning that Google didn't "read" it. I thanked him and walked back to my desk, recognizing that I'd learned something new today.

I finished the day feeling accomplished. I hadn't embarrassed myself. I hadn't succumbed to the giant bowl of M&Ms in the nook. I'd written the drafts of a bunch of outlines and had participated in more meetings in one day than I had in several years of freelancing. I left the office thinking, "I can do this."

The second day I took the outline information I'd created in a Word document and spent several hours adding all of the outlines I'd written for my first client into Excel, a program I'd only used once or twice before. I had to move my cursor into the right cell in the spreadsheet to be able to enter information into it, and it took a while to get the hang of it. Finally, I finished four outlines for my compressed air systems client and wound up deleting the entire spreadsheet. I tried to recover it, but it was gone.

"Shit," I muttered. I spent a few more minutes trying to "undo" in Excel before I gave up and walked across the office to Sean's desk. So far, he was the most techie person I'd met. I explained what had happened and asked if he could help me recover it.

Sean was puzzled. "You're not supposed to be using that spreadsheet yet," he said. "I haven't finished setting it up for you."

Frank had shown me where my spreadsheet would live on the server, and I'd found it that morning, opened it, and started filling it out (I mean, populating it) with my first outline. Then, I had deleted my morning's work and the template. "Oh, crud," I said. "I'm sorry! I didn't realize that."

Sean looked at me. "I'll let you know when it's set up," he said.

"Okay! Sounds good! Sorry again!" I scuttled back to my desk.

So much for my idea of showing initiative. How had I managed to delete something I wasn't even supposed to use yet? I went back to my Word document instead and continued working on outlines while I contemplated my mistake.

I marinated in my anxiety for a while before I got caught up in outlines again and was distracted by writing outlines about reclaimed wood furniture and stairs, basketball camps, and aircraft refurbishing. I went for a walk at lunchtime, relishing the opportunity to get out from under the fluorescent lights, and the rest of the day passed relatively quickly.

By the third day, though, I was beginning to wonder how long it would take before I felt like an employee, not like someone playing the part of an employee. I'd made the mistake of calculating my hourly rate that afternoon and realized that each day I sat at the office I was making about $160. I'd redone the math three times. Just $160? For an entire day's work? That couldn't be right. As a freelancer, my daily nut, or the number I tried to average ranged from $250 to $400, but I typically worked four to six hours in a day, with a goal of making $75-100/hour.

So, $20/hour was … demoralizing. You didn't take the job for the hourly rate, I reminded myself on the way home. It's health insurance, remember? And security.

I understood that I was trading time for money. That's what anyone who works does. What would sweeten the deal? Well, making more money, but that was off the table for the moment. What if I could work from home one day a week? Could I dream of two? That would give me some flexibility back, and some freedom. Why should I sit at my cubicle all day when could stretch out on my favorite corner of the couch, my feet on my ottoman, my cat on my lap, and a Netflix British murder series running in the background?

The next day I headed out at lunch for a 20-minute walk. It was sunny day in the 40s—a rarity for Chicago in January. "It's day four," I said to Polly, stepping carefully over a patch of mud on the sidewalk. "And no one has given me a plaque, award, trophy, or anything. What's up with that?"

"What? What's wrong with them? Maybe you'll get it tomorrow," Polly answered. "So, what's it like?"

"It's … okay," I said. "I realized I'm trading my time for money. And not much money." I filled her in on my discouraging realization from the day before. "So, I can either make more money, which isn't going to happen, or I can spend less time on the office. I'm going to work on the latter."

"Sounds smart." We chatted for a couple of minutes about her current book project and her hopes for it. That led us to talking about goals. I told her that the previous year, when I'd written down my goals (as I did every year), I'd included "being open to anything work-wise, even a 9-5 job." I'd forgotten that I'd written that until I'd revisited my goals over Christmas break. The universe, apparently, had not.

"Do you believe that?" I asked Polly. "That I manifested the job? Or at least helped to?"

"Hell, yeah! I always say, when you know the 'why,' the universe will provide the 'how,'" she said.

"Well, I thought my 'why' was health insurance," I said. "Now I'm starting to realize it's about managing my anxiety. I may be many things right now, but I'm not anxious." Discontented. Vaguely out of sorts. Somewhat bored. But some hours passed relatively quickly, like when I became absorbed in what I was reading, slurping down Wikipedia sites like smoothies.

Writing the outline for a bottling manufacturer, I stumbled onto "bottling," the term for when concert-goers pelt band members with, yes, bottles, and other items. Who knew? Performers ranging from Blink 182 to Justin Bieber to the Red Hot Chili Peppers had been bottled in the last decade. Researching custom socks for track and field athletes led to me reading about Marion Jones, who admitted to doping seven years after the fact and had her Olympic medals stripped as a result.

I loved to learn, and the job let me do that. And I was finding a pleasure in having a place to go every day. In kissing the kids goodbye and heading to Work. Even in pouring the first cup of coffee of the day into my wide-mouthed Digital Edge mug. I eavesdropped on the sales guys who sat around me and started to deepen my knowledge about what the company actually did and how the sales guys pitched and closed clients.

"He thought our web design capabilities weren't robust enough for his needs," said Marcus, the vice president of sales, referring to a client he hadn't been able to close. "So, he's using Square Space instead."

I listened, absorbed, and starting using the lingo. I used the word onboarding. I used the word metrics. I used the word populate. I realized that working might let me embrace my inner geek.

Because words are my thing. I like phrases like cognitive dissonance, woefully underemployed, and actively miserable (as opposed to passively miserable). Words matter. I have favorite quotes (just ask my kids), and at the beginning of every year, I choose a word to represent my overarching intention for the next 12 months. My word last year had been *open* while the word for 2019 was *deliberate*. Both the adjective and the verb. I wanted to be more conscious about my decisions and to consider all of my options before making a decision. I tended to react emotionally, instead of intellectually, and I wanted to change that if I could.

Top Ten Biz Speak Terms Heard Within the First Week (Thanks, Sales Guys!)

1. Onboarding
2. Metrics
3. Populate
4. Conversion
5. Migrate
6. Platform
7. Deliverables
8. SOW (statement of work)
9. Bandwidth
10. Metadata

With just a week into my tenure, Frank called me into a meeting. He told me then that the company was going to triple the number of clients that it transferred to Digital Plus. Over a time span of the next two months.

I took a breath and tried to be deliberate. I used another biz-speak term I'd heard a lot recently—metrics, as in, "what metrics will I be measured on?" (Note that in nearly 53 years, I had never uttered the word metrics. I hadn't even written it. I had said metric, as in the metric system, which the U.S.

briefly flirted with back in the 70s. But metrics, plural? Nope. January 9, 2019 was the first time. Ever.)

Frank's answer was brief. "Volume, quality, and efficiency." When I asked Frank to define "volume," he cautioned me about worrying about specific numbers. My position was the first ever at the company, so there were no parameters to measure my progress against. Anyone else would have thought, great! Instead, I worried. How would I know if I was doing a good job if I couldn't measure myself against a standard?

As a freelancer, that was easy—the amount of money I was making. If I was making $60,000, $80,000, or even $100,000, I had a daily nut—a specific amount I needed to make every day, five days a week. When I hit that number, I knew that I was on target. I could track my volume, but how would I know whether it was enough? And how to measure quality and efficiency? The former was subjective; the latter again required some kind of metrics (!!!) to calculate same.

I decided to keep track of my own production. I could then measure my own volume, and I might be able to determine how efficient I was over time. As for quality? I was less concerned about that as each outline was like writing a recipe. You named the page, provided the URL, what type of page it was (i.e., a home page, a landing page, a location page, a blog post), provided the keywords, wrote a summary of what the page was to contain, and provided resources. As long as I included the correct ingredients (i.e., keywords and resources) and my summary was clear and easy to understand, the recipe worked. The quality of the content itself was up to the writer who would create it, not me.

A few days later, I stopped by Sarah's desk after 3:00, when Frank left for the day. Sarah sat diagonally behind me, at a different six-pack, and had started a week after I did, but I hadn't had a chance to talk to her. I'd noticed that she wore cool cat's-eye glasses, colorful scarves, and was a few years older than me—a rarity at the company. I hoped we might have something in common.

"I know who you are!" she said, pointing at me. "I've read your books. I've freelanced, too."

"Wow!" I grinned. "Thank you!"

I never got tired of these fan moments, though they were more likely to happen at the writers' conference in New York that I attended every year. My books on freelancing hadn't been bestsellers but were midlist titles that still sold and attracted readers who wanted to make a living as full-time freelancers.

"So, what happened? Did you just get burned out on freelancing?" she asked. I liked that kind of directness—I'd learn later it was the reporter in her—and was surprised by it. Possibly because no one at Digital Edge, other than Frank, had bothered to ask why I'd wound up here. What for me was a huge shift in priorities and lifestyle was of no interest to anyone at work.

I wasn't ready to be honest with her. "It's not that I was burned out," I said. "This seemed like a good fit for me and having decent health insurance is a huge plus. And it's three miles from my house, which I can't beat! What about you?"

"Oh, I needed to get out of the house," she said, tucking one foot under as she settled back in her chair. "I needed a reset. I wasn't doing that much," and as she continued, I had that familiar flash of envy I experienced when I met a woman who didn't have to work.

For years I'd eyed the fit, toned moms in yoga pants who sat at Peet's sipping coffee and chatting for hours with apparently nothing they had to rush off to. I'd envied that kind of freedom even as I realized I didn't necessarily want it.

Work gave me meaning. Purpose. I liked the satisfaction of accomplishing assignments, of finishing a story, of turning in a particularly tricky book chapter. It had never been hard for me to make a deadline because missing one would not only cause me an incredible amount of cognitive dissonance (having never done so as a freelancer) but because missing one would also deny me of the pleasure of meeting said deadline.

I thrived on to-do lists, and on the idea of making progress, and tracking that progress — even if it was only the progress of meeting that day's goals. Meeting my daily nut was one way of doing that, as was accomplishing whatever I needed to do for the day.

Sarah had been an editor for publications including *The Wall Street Journal*, and more recently, *Patch*, a hyper-local community website. "So, you know all about the *Associated Press Stylebook*, then," I said, admitting that I was more familiar with *Chicago Manual of Style*, the stylebook most book publishers I worked with preferred.

"I'm brushing up on it now," she said, tapping the style guide on her desk. "There is a lot to learn here." We talked briefly about her position there as editor. She was given a list of pieces to edit—landing pages, blog posts, content assets (off-site infographics and guest blogs that were published on other websites, not the clients')–called the "queue" by Frank every morning. As she edited them, she turned them in to Frank, who then sent them on to the account manager, or AM, who shared them with the client for feedback. If the client approved a piece of content, it was then sent on the web developer who uploaded the page to the client's site, or to the content marketing specialist (or CMS, not to be confused with the company's other CMS, the content management system), who looked for a website to publish it as a backlink.

Backlinks were a sometimes-overlooked aspect of building an SEO campaign. A backlink is the term for when another site links to yours, driving traffic there. Google considers the number of backlinks a site has, and the quality of those backlinks (i.e., are the sites legitimate websites or have they been created simply as "link farms"), and takes that into account when determining how high your site will rank on a search.

After I finished chatting with Sarah, I headed back to my desk, and checked my personal email to discover the bill for Haley's after-school care was due. I logged on to the site, paid the fee, and then had a surge of money anxiety. I was going to be making barely enough to cover my bills, and childcare for Haley was one cost I had underestimated.

Deep breaths. Deep breaths. This was how I got into an anxious spiral. I chanted one of my abundance mantras. "There is enough money. There always has been enough money. There will always be enough money." When I remembered, I started my day with affirmations, most of which centered around trying to attract what I wanted (meaningful work, enough money, fewer intrusive thoughts about money or whether I was a decent mom or whether Walt and I had a future together, you name it). While my spiritual beliefs were never crystalline, I did believe that focusing on good things was likely to attract good things and that focusing on my worries never helped. I mentally stroked myself back into a place of, if not grace, slight contentment, and resolved to continue what I was doing — monitoring my spending and not making myself nuts about the money going out the door.

In the meantime, I'd continue with my deep breaths — and hope not to breathe so deeply I wound up passing out.

The Corporate Newbie's Cheat Sheet: Starting Your New Job (Yay!)

You're about to start your new job. Woo hoo! You're likely nervous, anxious, worried about making a good first impression. Here's some advice for your first day.

First off, do a trial run of what your commute will look like, and give yourself plenty of time to get to the office a few minutes early. Choose an outfit that makes you feel confident, smart, attractive. (Because you are! You got this!) Get a blowout the day before, or get your nails done. You want to walk in feeling smashing.

I also suggest bringing some emergency snacks in your purse. A protein bar, a bag of nuts, a banana. I wasn't used to sitting at a desk all day when my kitchen wasn't ten feet away if I got hungry. Don't let your first day be spent hangry because you didn't have enough for breakfast.

You'll meet a lot of people your first few days. Shake hands. Make eye contact. Smile. Ask people what they do. Then at your desk, write down their names (on a seating chart, if you have one) and any information they gave you. It will help you get people's names down, which will help you acclimate more quickly (hopefully!)

Look for the helpers, as Mr. Rogers liked to say. Note who seems genuinely welcoming and who tells you to come to him or her with questions, because you will have them. And if you can't figure out how to do something, Google that shit before you ask your boss or anyone else for help. But don't flail around for hours when a quick explanation from your coworker may give you the answer you need.

Finally, recognize that your first few days, or likely weeks, you're going to feel awkward and unsure and sometimes stupid. That's normal. It's part of starting a new job. Suck it up and make sure you give yourself plenty of downtime at home, if possible. In a few weeks, you'll settle in and much of what you may be struggling with (like finding documents on the company server or figuring out how to contact your company's tech support department) will be automatic.

CHAPTER 3

Scalability

Monday morning, I was running late but made it to work with five minutes to spare. Score! I got coffee, sat down, and immediately started working on outlines. I was full of Monday morning enthusiasm—I'd done little the weekend before except laze around with Walt at his quiet, dark little house (which I referred to as the sensory deprivation tank to my friends), watching network TV, reading the paper, and thinking about how little we had in common and that we should probably just accept that we weren't meant to be together, simply break up, and move on. We'd been dating for a year, but because of the distance between us and the fact that I was a fulltime parent, our relationship seemed to have stalled out. We loved each other. We had fun together. And there was no move by either of us to take the relationship any further.

I'd been ticking off the hours until I could leave his house to meet the kids at home, but he'd surprised me by coming on to me as we were lying on the couch watching TV. He started kissing me and then pulled me against him, unzipping my jeans to slide his hand between my legs. He touched me gently, continuing to kiss me. I felt that tiny pilot light of desire suddenly whoosh into a flame, and we were yanking each other's clothes off.

I'd started to say something, amazed at how good I felt, and he interrupted me by kissing me hard. "Fuck me," he'd growled. "Just fuck me." I complied.

Afterward, I lay on the couch with my feet in his lap, sated, and happy. Walt pointed out his 80+-year-old neighbor was outside shoveling snow. "She probably heard you," he said.

"She probably thinks you were murdering me," I grinned at him. "And I don't even care."

I didn't. It had been a while since we'd had the kind of sex where I forgot myself. Where I forgot everything. I still wanted that. I needed it.

"Remind me of why we're not going to have sex?" I'd asked him on our second date. We'd gone out for burgers, and then I'd taken him to Q, the pool hall where I played in an 8-ball league every week to shoot. I'd liked him enough, even then, to bring him to one of what I called my petri dishes. He was a good pool player, slow and methodical. When one of my 20-something teammates (yes, another Millennial) texted me, I wound up inviting her to join us, temporarily forgetting that I was on a date. He didn't mind, but Sam was mortified.

"Wait a minute!" she'd said as I introduced Walt. "Are you guys ... on a date?"

"Well, yeah," I admitted. "But it's no big deal."

Walt was holding his pool cue. "Yeah, it's no big deal," he said. "Besides, I've always wanted to have a threesome," he said to me but loud enough so she could hear. "And she's cute."

"Walt!" I knew he was joking.

Sam did, too, and laughed. "You old people are so weird."

The three of us hung out for several hours. Walt was sweet and relaxed. He seemed not at all perturbed at the fact that our date had turned into a threesome, albeit a very tame one.

"I like him!" Sam had yelled at me in the bathroom after several beers.

"I like him, too," I admitted, washing my hands.

"No, I like him for *you*."

"I like him for me, too! Relax!" I'd laughed.

I'd liked him even more that night, when we were kissing on my couch and despite me pressing my body against him, my intent clear, he hadn't put his hands on me. He'd briefly touched my breast with the tips of his fingers, and I'd tensed, but he had stopped there.

"Why aren't we having sex right now?" I'd asked him between kisses, only half-joking.

"I've had too many relationships that were about sex. I want more than that with you," he said, stroking my shoulder. "I really like you."

"I know. You're right." But I wanted him. I'd wanted him since I noticed his big, scarred hands on the bar on our first encounter, which I'd decided to call an actual date on the drive back home. When he'd finally kissed me three hours later, in the parking lot, eagerly, hungrily, I'd wanted him even more.

This was different from what I'd felt with Richard. I hadn't been ready to have sex with Richard, but I'd capitulated to get it out of the way and out of a desire to please him, to make him like me. With Walt, my desire overrode logic. I'd asked him to lie down with me and cuddle, knowing what was likely to happen. We'd lain there in the near-dark, our bodies pressed together, and he still had done nothing more than kiss me. The kind of kissing I'd forgotten about. Feeling the warmth of his body, his mouth on mine, his arms around me, I hadn't been able to stop myself. I'd muttered, "I can't take this anymore," somehow yanked off his jeans and my own, straddling him in one smooth motion I would never be able to replicate.

Our connection had been powerful, and for a few minutes my mind had been emptied of anything except my desire for him. Afterward, I went to the bathroom to pee and clean up. He stopped me before I got back into bed.

"Can I ask you to do something for me?"

"Um … okay."

"Will you turn the light on and let me look at you?"

I closed my eyes. "Really?"

"Please?"

"Okay." I sighed and turned on the light. He was lying on his side, his head propped up on his hand. He looked into my eyes, and then his eyes traveled down my body before returning to my face.

"You. Are. Beautiful."

One good thing about being middle-aged? Sometimes, you know what not to say. So, I didn't say, "No, I'm not," "I have cellulite everywhere," or "you're only saying that because you just got laid."

Instead, I said, "thank you," even though I didn't believe him. I shut off the light and crawled back into bed, scooting my body closer to him.

"By the way, you're spending the night," I said, poking him in the arm. I wanted to feel him next to me all night, to wake up to him in the morning. Richard had never done that though I'd asked him more than once.

Walt had wrapped his arms around me and pulled me against his solidness. "Where else would I go?" he'd murmured. He'd fallen asleep almost immediately, his breath warm against my neck. I'd surprised myself by relaxing into his arms and falling asleep almost as easily, only to wake in the middle of the night, aware of his body next to me. He'd woken up, too, and we'd kissed, talked, and laughed in the dark, the only two people in the world for a few brief hours.

I didn't regret having sex with him so quickly. I needed the intimacy and, even more, the respite from the rest of my life.

When we had sex, my overly anxious, continually analyzing/assessing/evaluating brain shut off, at least for a while. The physical release was part of it but even more than that was the connection I felt. It drove my desire for him.

Walt sometimes joked I used him for sex, and lately I'd started to suspect that he was having sex with me not because he wanted to but because he thought I wanted to. Or because I hadn't come the last time we had. Or because I came on to him—I did that a lot—and he didn't want to say no. And the sex … well, they say sex is like pizza and even bad sex isn't that bad. But I'd had enough sex to know that that's not actually true.

It was never flat-out terrible, but it sometimes felt like he wasn't present. He was hard, his cock was inside me, he might be kissing me or touching me, but he didn't feel there. I'd told him I'd rather not have sex than to have it when he wasn't 100 percent wanting to.

"But I know you need it sometimes. It helps your anxiety," he countered.

"I know. And I appreciate that. But it's so much better when you want to," I said. "I can feel the difference." I missed how it had been at the beginning. The way he kissed me, deep and slow, his mouth fastened on mine when he was inside me. The way he looked at me when he was pulling off my panties. The way he talked to me. He was sweet sometimes, other times crude—and I sopped it all up and rediscovered that loose easiness you feel after sex that is both intense and tender.

But was that enough? I had debated whether to put a picture of us up on my cubicle wall. Did I want to announce to the work world that I was, well, "taken"? The fact that it even crossed my mind revealed that I didn't have both feet in my relationship, but I went ahead and tacked up a picture of the two of us from a trip to Milwaukee next to pictures of Ryan and Haley. He had his arm around me, and we looked relaxed and happy.

Later that morning, I realized I'd sent the wrong outlines to Roger. I had two working versions of the spreadsheet, one that was saved on the company server and the other that was saved to my desktop. I'd created and saved the latter version to keep copies of some earlier drafts of outlines but then accidentally created the new outlines on my personal version, which, in short, meant that they weren't saved to the company server version, which meant that Roger had accessed the wrong ones. Which meant that I had made a mistake—a stupid one—and that Roger had done work for nothing, wasting at least 20-30 minutes of his time.

I swore under my breath, apologized to Roger, and double-checked the other outlines to make sure that I'd saved the most recent versions in the master server, not my backup. I had, and I moved on. But I was aware of my urge to apologize again.

Jesus, I'd made a mistake. Let it go. How many times had I heard Haley sing the theme from *Frozen*? Roger was gracious about it, and I didn't need to flog myself any longer. Later that morning, I sent my notes for an outline to an account manager, or AM, per Frank's direction. This client wanted to do its own writing, so we wouldn't be using an in-house or freelance writer. The AM sent me a frosty email complaining about the brevity of my notes and asking for a more "client-facing" document.

The AMs all worked out of the Atlanta office, but I'd met this one in person briefly the week before when she was in town. Yet, her tone sounded … well, snotty. She knew I'd been here less than two weeks, right? I was debating how to respond when Frank called my name over his shoulder.

"Don't reply to that email," he said. "I'm doing it." I hadn't realized that he had been cc'd on it as well. His response rolled into my email a couple of minutes later. It was measured but direct. He explained that the notes I had sent were what the writer would typically receive and that if she had specific suggestions about how to improve the process for her to let him know.

My gut reaction had been to pick up the phone, apologize (of course!), and ask her for feedback/direction. I'd always found that it's better to call someone than to try to address something like this by email or text. It inevitably devolved. After all, the way you read an email was often dependent on your mood at the moment. When I felt irritable or tired, I could read a snotty tone into just about any communication. That's why phone was better.

But Frank had gone to bat for me—and before I could handle it my way. I was grateful—and bothered. I thought my gut reaction—to immediately call her to clarify and resolve the situation—had been the right one.

We talked about it later in Yahoo. "Do you agree with me about the tone of her email?" he asked.

"Well, yeah. I felt a bit like I'd been bitch-slapped." As usual, my words got ahead of me. "Sorry. It made me feel like I wanted to take my toys and go home."

"That's why I jumped in," he said. "You haven't even been here for two weeks. I've been here for years, and you'll find out that sometimes people want us to do their jobs for them. I don't want you to be taken advantage of, and I thought her tone was out of line."

I agreed, but I didn't want my boss stepping in for me. It felt too paternal. I missed my dad sometimes, but I didn't need another one. "I do appreciate what you did," I said. "But in the future, are you willing to let me handle it my way?"

He leaned back in his chair. "What would you have done?"

"Picked up the phone," I replied. "Talk to her. Resolve the issue. I mean, I'm the new person here but I'm going to have to work with the AMs and that means creating relationships with them. If you jump in for me, that may get in the way of doing that."

Frank thought for a minute. "I can appreciate that."

"Don't get me wrong. I appreciate you stepping in for me as the new girl here," I said. "But I'd like to be able to handle issues like this that arise my way. If I need your help, I will certainly ask."

He agreed, and we moved on. I figured the next time I had an encounter with her, I'd go out of my way to facilitate a relationship. I wasn't sure how much contact I'd have with the AMs, but I did have to reach out to them with questions about their clients that I couldn't answer on my own, even with the help of Google.

I still felt a nagging discomfort about the AM that made me question whether I was worried about creating and maintaining positive working relationships with my coworkers—or whether I simply wanted everyone to like me.

Both were, in fact, true.

I was going to have to work with her in the weeks and months to come if I managed to stick it out at this job. I valued relationships, and I wanted to start off making a positive impression with the people I worked with, especially those from whom I would need information to be able to do my job in the future.

It was the first recognition that no matter how friendly, no matter how team-oriented, no matter how positive, connected, and rah-rah our company might be, there was always going to be some amount of drama. That was simply part of the work, something that I had forgotten about during my years of freelancing. So far, I was getting along with everyone, but my conversations were limited to the smallest of small talk and saying hello to everyone I encountered in the nook or on the way to the bathroom or back. Still, I felt like I was playing the role of an employee and wondered when I'd feel like I was truly part of the place.

A few mornings later, Frank called a meeting in Yahoo to inform me that my workload was about to double. I was currently responsible for creating outlines for about 50 clients. Another 50 or so would be transferred over to the Digital Plus platform in the next month, and 50 more the month after. So, actually, my workload was actually going to triple.

I'd been working steadily every day, confident that I could handle the amount of work I'd been given. I was producing, on average 16 to 20 outlines a day for 4 to 6 clients. Frank was assigning me writing tasks as well. Sometimes, outlines took longer than expected or there was a lot of back and forth with SEO about keywords that slowed my speed. I could probably do double the amount of work. But triple? There. Was. No. Way.

Before I could go into full-on freak-out mode, however, Frank spoke. "We realize that we don't yet know how much you can handle," said Frank. "The intent is to hire someone under you to help out."

Oh. Okay. Without even digesting that, I launched into something that had been on my mind. "I just want you to know that I really like working here. There have been a few ups and downs, but I do like coming to work and working with you and the rest of the content team. I'm excited about being here," I said. "There are only two things that could make this job more palatable to me—more money, which I realize is off the table for now, or more freedom and flexibility. I was going to wait to tell you this, but I'm letting you know that I'm going to ask to work from home one or two days a week, starting this summer and continuing after that. I think you can tell already that I don't need anyone standing over me to make sure that I get my work done. "And," I added, shrugging, "that would give me the best of both worlds."

Frank's response was measured. "I do have a writer who works offsite for reasons that are between him and me," he said. "And I let Evie work from home sometimes. There are times when you will need to talk to Sean or someone else and you can walk over, but you can do that with email." I wasn't sure what he was thinking, but he didn't say no. I was heartened.

I returned to work, churning out a few more outlines, and mentally patted myself on the back for being direct. For asking for what I wanted. My confidence didn't last, though. The next day, I discovered that I'd produced outlines for a client for which the keywords had not been approved and sent them on to Roger, who had processed them and sent them on to Frank to be assigned to writers. As I explored further, I realized I'd done the same with 12 additional outlines for several more clients, without confirming keyword approval.

When I apologized to Roger and explained what had happened, he said something about having plenty to do without having to process outlines which were not approved. That, combined with the fact that I had screwed up, repeatedly, triggered an emotional response.

I was an idiot. I had wasted not only my time but also Roger's time and Frank's time. Dammit. I was taking deep breaths at my desk when Frank called an impromptu meeting and asked Roger and me to join him in Yahoo. My eyes were filling with tears as we walked toward the room. Do not cry. Do not fucking cry, I told myself. But I was tired. I was overwhelmed. I was a girl. I blinked back the tears that were brimming on my eyelids, mentally willing them back into my tear ducts. Nonetheless, it was clear that I was upset.

It was hard to say who was more uncomfortable. Me, trying not to cry, or the two men in their late 50s sitting with a woman who was trying not to cry.

I apologized again to Roger for the extra work and attempted to take deep, steadying-yet-subtle breaths. My face was hot, and my heart was pounding. We walked through what had happened and how to avoid it in the future. I managed to get better (some, anyway) control over my emotions. Frank told Roger that was all he needed from him.

"We're all learning here," said Frank. "Eventually this process is going to improve. In six months—if you're still here in six months—you'll see how much better this will be. We're figuring things out right now; think about your mental health."

I gulped and nodded, struggling to get my emotions under control. I managed to leave the meeting without actually crying, but my throat ached. I wanted to be anywhere but work. I walked back to my desk, immersed myself in outlines, and made it through the rest of the day without even a minor mental breakdown.

A few days later, Frank asked to meet to discuss the person he'd be hiring to work with me. Writing skills were on the top of the list of attributes he was looking for. "First off, plenty of people can't even communicate verbally, but if you do have someone who can do that, often they can't write," he said. "You should see the emails I get. Even resumes and writing samples. They have spelling mistakes. And these are their writing samples! We can teach some things, but there's a difference between teaching someone and babysitting them."

Even if a candidate had decent writing samples, he or she could wow you in an interview and then fail to deliver, like the writer Frank had hired who'd been late four out of five mornings his first week of work. Frank and I were the proverbial preacher and choir. Both type As, both deadline-driven, both self-motivated to the point of stress-induced heart attacks, as the studies prove. But it's type As that get things done.

We continued talking about how difficult it can be to determine whether someone will turn out to be … well, a worker. Someone who would step up and tackle whatever was offered to him or her. Someone willing to learn. Someone able to learn. I had learned plenty of new skills since I'd started. Before Digital Edge, I'd only used Excel to create invoices for one client, who insisted upon them. Now I was populating them like a badass. I was getting the hang of Workfront, which was like a business version of Facebook. I could now navigate around the company server without having to ask Frank where to find documents.

Frank had said that I would train whoever we hired, and I was excited at the idea of having someone to work with, not simply next to. I'd expected a more collaborative environment, but except the sales guys, there was little camaraderie. About half of the office sat with headphones on, and people tended to sit at their cubes unless they were on their way to the bathroom or the nook for coffee or yet another plastic-packaged snack. I brought my lunch every day but had already succumbed to Twizzlers, peanut-butter-and-cheese crackers, and packaged cookies more than once.

Frank showed me the job description, which was for a "junior content specialist." I wasn't sure what the "junior" designation meant except that maybe that meant entry-level. I wondered what the salary would be—it would presumably be less than the $35,000 I'd originally been offered. Maybe $25,000/year? Who knew? That was another caveat I'd come across in the employee manual—that any discussion of salary other than with your manager made you subject to termination.

I'd never seen this kind of language before, even as a lawyer who handled small business and employment issues. To me, this clause suggested two things: that first off, some people were getting paid a lot of money, and that other people (more likely, a lot of people) were not. I could only guess at what salaries might be in different departments. How could you quantify the value of, say, the internet marketing specialist, who determined whether incoming calls or emails were potential customers, compared to, say, a content marketing specialist, who created backlinks for clients? What about the SEO team, who determined what the appropriate keywords for each page of content would be? And the dev team, who implemented new content?

During my interview, I'd seen the job descriptions for the position of content specialist and editor with the relevant salaries attached. I could only guess at what salary ranges might be for other positions, but I figured the sales team and the account managers probably made the most money. After all, the sales team sold the clients on the company, and the AMs were responsible for keeping those clients happy—and keeping them as clients. A lot of clients signed 6-month or 12-month contracts. If their SEO campaigns didn't deliver results, clients moved on. That meant the sales guys always had to produce to make up for attrition and that AMs were also always trying to extend contracts or "increase the spend," the amount a client paid for its SEO (or PPC) campaign each month. We had clients who paid as little as $500/month and clients who paid $10,000 or more; the amount they spent determined the size of the campaign, including the amount of content that we'd produce for the client. The higher the budget, the more content would be expected.

In addition to creating outlines, Frank had begun giving me actual writing assignments. The first was a home page for a company that specialized in interior repairs, nondestructive testing, and window repairs on commercial and corporate aircraft. My work on the page wasn't Pulitzer-worthy by any means, but it matched the tone of the current site, addressed every point in the outline, and gave me a break from the minutiae of creating outlines.

It felt good to be back in my comfort zone, creating service-oriented copy with readers in mind. It was a reminder that I wanted to do more writing, not just create recipes for other writers. I let Frank know that I was eager to take on more writing work and hoped he would assign me more.

In the meantime, reality was starting to dawn. Namely that a certain amount of boredom is part of any job. I was actually caught up on work and was waiting on SEO to give me keyword approval so I could move forward with outlines. I didn't like sitting around with nothing to do and was tempted to walk over and gently pester Seth, the SEO manager, and the rest of his team.

But I didn't. About 15 years prior, I'd worked for Pampered Chef on a freelance basis. I was hired to fill in for two employees in the marketing department, both of whom were on maternity leave. The manager had originally wanted me to work five days a week, but we agreed on an hourly rate ($55/hour) and working three days a week.

The first few days, I was thrilled by the idea of working again. I got up, showered, dressed in grown-up clothes, and joined the traffic heading north on I-355 to the office in Addison, a suburb about 20 minutes north of me. I felt a solidarity with all of these other workers, all driving to our destinations where we would contribute to the gross national product, to society, and to the world in general. It was heady. It was exciting. It was fun. It … lasted about two weeks.

I was "tasked" (ugh, more business-speak) with writing articles for the Kitchen Consultant newsletters. The pieces were short—often between 75 and 250 words—about the uses of the Pampered Chef product line, how to host effective "Kitchen Shows" (we never used the term *parties*), boost your sales numbers, and more. It was service journalism wrapped up in a corporate marketing package, and I was good with that. I churned out articles that were then sent up the line through no fewer than four levels of edits and approvals before they could be signed off on by the vice president of marketing.

The stories were simple to write, and short, pithy, service-y pieces are my thing. One morning, maybe a week into my position there, I bounced over to my boss' desk, a sweet, hard-working woman in her late 20s. "Hey! I need more work," I told her. I'd spent the last couple of hours writing seven or eight of these short pieces, directing them to the relevant editors, and answering a few minor questions about other pieces in the meantime.

"What about the other pieces I gave you?"

"Those are all done, too." I probably sounded smug or flippant, but that wasn't my intention. I was used to cranking out work, as fast as I could, and then rewarding myself with downtime. I was hyper-focused on my billable rate, or what I made per-hour, and that meant that I strived for efficiency. That served me well as a freelancer, but in a corporate setting, as the lone freelancer, it was only highlighting the fact that:

1. I worked faster—much faster — than anyone else on the team.

And its corollary:

2. The team members worked slower—much slower—than I did.

It took me a little while to realized that I needed to slow down. Way down. I needed to adapt to my corporate environment instead of expecting it to adapt to me. I intentionally slowed my pace and looked for ways to kill time during my eight-hour shifts there.

So, when I was sitting at my desk contemplating how many hours were left to sit on my butt, I didn't walk over to SEO to prod them. Instead, I took long, slow, deep breaths, reminded myself that I was having an adventure, and decided to research corporate productivity while thinking about workplace-acceptable (I hoped) ways to waste time.

Workplace-Acceptable Ways to Waste Time (and Hopefully Make the Day Go by More Quickly)

1. Walk more slowly.
2. Drink more coffee/tea/water. (Bonus: this will also mean that you will be urinating more frequently, so you'll have to take more time for bathroom breaks, during which you will practice your slower style of walking.)
3. Become OCD-level clean with your handwashing. (Bonus points for bringing hand lotion to rub into your skin which is now dry and chapped from all that handwashing.)
4. Each time you're in the bathroom (and that will be a lot of times), consider your current hairstyle choice. Rate its pros and cons. Or simply take an extra minute to note all of the new lines and wrinkles that you didn't notice in the bathroom mirror this morning.

5. Take several minutes to breathe deeply before you tackle any task. Then, breathe deeply after its conclusion. Your coworkers may think you're becoming a Buddhist, but that's okay.

6. Instead of sticking with one task (and getting more done), jump from task to task to task. Populate your spreadsheet with a line or two of data. Then, check your email. Visit your LinkedIn profile. Update your latest project list. Back to the spreadsheet, then back to email, and repeat. You won't get much done, but an outside observer will see an illusion of busy-ness and productivity.

7. Remind yourself that time is an illusion. Mentally list your favorite bands from college. List your boyfriends. The guys you ever liked. The guys you kissed. The guys you never got to kiss. Your most memorable runs.

8. Google shit. Exercises to improve your golf swing. How to save for retirement. How to not go broke in retirement. How to determine whether you'll go broke in retirement. Holistic treatments for anxiety. How to stop stress-eating. How to not gain weight during menopause. Pros and cons of marriage in midlife. How to raise resilient, independent kids. Recipes with five ingredients or fewer that take ten minutes or fewer to cook. With any luck, you'll become so absorbed that you'll discover that 15, even 30, minutes have elapsed.

9. List everything you're grateful for, including your kids, your health, your guy, the fact you're a little less anxious than you were a month ago. The fact that even at 52, you can still run (although slowly) four miles. That you have great friends. That you're

leasing a car that has doors and windows that actually work, unlike your former 19-year-old (much-beloved) Honda.

10. Practice mindfulness. Bring your mind to the moment. Ground yourself to the earth through your feet. Note that nothing in your physical body hurts and add that to your gratitude list. Check your watch and note that another three minutes have passed, and remind yourself that you are not actively miserable at this precise moment.

Three weeks in, and some aspects of the job were getting easier. I hadn't been late to work (though I'd come close a couple of mornings); I was navigating my spreadsheets and other documents on the server with ease; and I'd nailed the names of about half of the people in the office by surreptitiously using my seating chart and writing notes on it to help distinguish between all the white guys wearing sweatshirts. Surely, this was progress.

So what if I was bored sometimes? So what if I was starting to hate the buzz of the florescent overheads? So what if I wasn't following my bliss? I was an adult, and this was adulting. Making yourself show up for shit you don't necessarily want to do. At dinner a few nights before, I'd asked the kids why I had taken this job. "Considering what you say when you get home from work, I don't know why you took this job," said Ryan, shoving pasta into his mouth.

"Yeah, Mom," said Haley, chiming in as always. "Why did you take the job?"

"Well, some days I don't know why I took it, either," I admitted. "But remember, health insurance. And I know I'm making a steady amount of money, and that that money is coming in, no matter what. And I do like the people I work with. But some of the time I'm bored. That's called having a job. Sometimes, it's boring even when you love what you do," I added.

Were they absorbing this life lesson? Who knew? I'd had 13 years of parenting experience at this point, and yet some days the idea of another 10 ½ years of heavy lifting seemed overwhelming, especially when I started thinking of all the dinners I'd have to make.

I knew family dinners were important. Kids who had family dinners did better in school. They were less likely to use drugs, less likely to get in disciplinary or legal trouble, and less likely to be violent. They had fewer psychological problems.

Still, some nights I wanted anything but to feed the children—feed them something nutritious and wholesome and satisfying—sit with them, spur Ryan to tell me something, anything, about his day, keep Haley from interrupting him, listen to Haley ramble on about her latest third grade girl drama while Ryan rolled his eyes and then interrupted her, to encourage Haley to eat more of her broccoli, Brussels sprouts, carrots, or whatever else was the healthiest item on her plate and keep their everyday bickering from morphing into a full-blown battle, and then to listen to them argue about whose turn it was to clean up the dishes. Did I love them? For certain. Were there nights when I'd prefer to lie lifelessly on the couch while shoving something salty in my mouth and watching a British murder mini-series? Just as certainly.

The Corporate Newbie's Cheat Sheet: Making a Mistake at Work

You made your first mistake at work! Or maybe your second, or third. What do you do next? Well, if you're me, you likely swear, contemplate crying, and probably do cry, at least a little. These are not particularly useful responses to a screw-up.

Instead, take a few deep breaths and get your emotions under control. This is easier to do in private, so take a bathroom break or a five-minute walk around the building's parking lot. Talk yourself off of the ledge. What's the worst-case scenario here? You get fired? Was it that big of a mistake? Probably not. You just did something stupid, and you don't like feeling (or looking) stupid. Welcome to Earth!

Once you've calmed down, assess your mistake. Was it a biggie or something minor? How did it happen? Can you determine why you made the mistake (you didn't proofread an email, you attached the wrong file, or you had the wrong information)? Knowing why it happened will let you help prevent it from happening again.

Now, you've got to own it. Let the person who may be affected by the mistake (i.e., the person you sent the wrong file to) know that you screwed up, and apologize. Don't go overboard with the mea culpas. Own what you did, apologize, and rectify, like so: "Hey, Nat! I'm sorry—I attached the wrong file this morning. I've attached the correct file and apologize for any inconvenience. Thank you!"

The sweeping majority of people will think it's no big deal, accept your apology, and move on, and you should, too. If it's a huge, sweeping, giant screw-up? Same rules apply. Own it, apologize, rectify the situation, and do everything you can not to make the same mistake again. Do you need to start double-checking a file before you attach it? Or slow down to make sure you're emailing the correct "Bob" in the company because there are six of them? Figure out a strategy to lessen the chance of making that same mistake again, and move on.

CHAPTER 4

Metrics

At work, no one was praising me or showering me with positive feedback, but I was used to working as a freelancer, where compliments are rare. If an editor wasn't happy with something I'd written, she'd ask for revisions. If something looked good, the piece was accepted (sometimes I got a "nice job on this"), but I was accustomed to working without a lot of feedback.

That doesn't mean I don't like feedback. So, when Roger emailed to tell me that the client had approved a landing page I'd written on interior airline refurbishing—a subject I'd known nothing about—with only one minor change, I glowed.

Had I made the word a better place? Did it matter in the big picture or even in a smaller picture? Nope. Yet, that small amount of positive feedback kept me going through a demanding day. It wasn't ego as much as the sense of connection that positive feedback gave me. Nothing made me feel better than an authentic conversation or a shared laugh. I liked to connect, thrived on it, in fact, and I looked for ways to make it happen, whether it was giving a genuine compliment to a stranger, sending a carefully chosen card to a friend, or making an intention bracelet for someone who might appreciate one.

Last year I'd bought an intention bracelet for myself with the word *open* on it. It was a simple piece of knotted string with a washer-sized piece of metal that featured a word of your choice. I loved the idea of essentially tattooing a word on the inside of my wrist with none of the permanence (or pain).

Better still, you could buy a "maker's kit" and create the bracelets yourself. After I ponied up 70 dollars, I started making them for friends. I made one for Dana, a bartender I knew (*breathe*), for Chris (*love*), for my friend Lisa, who had recently been diagnosed with breast cancer (*grace*). When I found out someone I knew was having a hard time—whether that was a divorce, health issues, or other struggles, I'd email or text the person, ask for a word that had significance or meaning to him or her, and then get to work.

I sent each with a note that said:

"Similar to a prayer shawl, the idea of an intention bracelet is that its maker infuses it with prayers, positive energy, good vibes, you name it. That's what I've done in creating this for you. I hope it is a source of hope [or reminder that you are loved, or strength] in the days to come."

Each bracelet cost about six dollars for the overpriced supplies, but it was an easy way for me to help someone, or at least let her know I cared. That sense of connection and community was something I'd hoped to create at work, but a month in, that hadn't happened, at least not yet. However, I did have some place to go. Of course, every time I thought this, visions of Richard Gere in *An Officer and a Gentleman* intruded—"I got nowhere else to go! I got nowhere else!"— but I was starting to appreciate the routine.

Frank had asked me to meet with Melissa, a candidate for the junior content specialist position, after he interviewed her, to give her a better sense of the job. When I knocked on the door of Yahoo, they were just finishing up.

"Wow, I should have known you had an interview today," I teased Frank, who was wearing a sweater and chinos instead of his usual sweatshirt and jeans. "You've got your grown-up clothes on."

Frank rolled his eyes. "I'll leave you to it," he said, and I turned to Melissa. She was in her early 20s, pretty, with long dark hair and solidly built frame. She was wearing a blouse and dress pants, and 3" heels that looked like they hurt. A sign she wanted the job. We spoke briefly about the position and her background. I asked her whether she was an introvert or extrovert, and she seemed unsure of how to answer.

"I'm an extrovert in an introvert's job," I explained. "If you like human conversation, that's a good thing because we sit with the sales guys, and they actually talk. Plenty of people in the office don't seem to speak at all." I paused, realized I wasn't exactly selling Digital Edge. "Umm ... I can say I came here after being self-employed for more than 20 years, and it's not a bad place to work." She probably didn't need to know that I was primarily here for health insurance and (hopefully) a respite for my anxiety. Oh, and a place to go. Melissa had a couple of questions for me, and I answered as best I could.

"You've probably already figured out I'm a pretty transparent person," I said. "I tend to say what's on my mind. If you do work here, I'll do what I can to help you get up to speed. It's truly not a bad place to start your career if you're interested in content. You do get to learn a lot about a whole bunch of different things. Things you had no idea even existed or had any interest in. Like ball bearings. Compressed air systems. Refrigerated packing material." I held up my hand and smiled. "Seriously, it's not a bad job. I've been here for more than a month, and I'm still here!" I laughed, and she did, too, though it might have been out of politeness.

Apparently, I didn't scare her off because she accepted the job and would start in several weeks. Frank emailed me to let me know her start date and that she would work the same hours as me. "She wants to be your mini-me," he emailed.

"Smart girl!" I emailed back. I had already realized that Frank's preferred method of communication was email. Even though he sat just a few feet away from me, he would email even quick questions when I'd be more likely to turn in my chair, and say, "Hey, boss, question for you." I'd wait until I had his attention and then ask him what I needed to know.

While I liked face-to-face communication with other humans, I recognized that most of my coworkers appeared to prefer using their keyboards and had decided to respect that. I'd also been introduced to Slack, which employees used to instant message each other. I'd figured out that Slack was not only the name of the software but a verb, as in "I'll Slack you her contact info," or "Slack me when you get off that call." I continued to eavesdrop on the sales guys, envious of their easy camaraderie and their seemingly inexhaustible knowledge of SEO strategies and business speak. I was slowly being able to follow their conversations, realizing that I now understood more of what they were saying, like learning a foreign language where incomprehensible sounds suddenly announce themselves in your brain as actual words.

The sales guys were also the people in the office who dressed up for work. I knew when they had in-person meetings because they'd sport dress shirts and slacks, occasionally even jackets and ties for important potential clients. The rest of the office emphasized the casual.

I hadn't done that. I'd decided at the outset to dress like a grownup, which for me usually meant a wrap dress with platforms or wedges. I had lived in jeans and overalls for years as a freelancer, but I liked to feel pulled-together, even pretty, when I left for work. My appearance still mattered to me, even while I was fighting gravity, sun damage, the body shifts brought on by perimenopause, and the other inevitable aspects of aging. I knew what might be acceptable or even cute on a girl of 24 looked sloppy or unkempt on a woman of a certain age.

I talked about it with my friend Jill, my former research assistant, that night. She'd worked for me in college, and then done the corporate thing for years before opting to freelance a few years back. She and I got together for lunch every couple of months, commiserating about the ups and downs of freelancing, but I hadn't spoken to her since I'd started at Digital Edge.

"I'm dressing for the job I want," I told her. "Only I don't know what that job is. Just that it pays more." I sighed. "I don't know. Today I hate my job."

"Why?"

"I'm bored. I hate sitting there all day." I heard myself whining but didn't care. "I have to sit there *all* day! Even when I'm caught up with work. You know, when I was freelancing, I could work and then be done for the day."

"Yes, well, that is what a job entails," Jill gently pointed out. "You've been there more than a month, and you said you've only had two or three days where you hate your job, right? That's pretty good."

She was right. "I'll tell you one thing, though," I said. "I've been too transparent, telling him how much I like my job and how much I like working here. Those days are over."

"I agree," Jill said. "Why are you even saying that?"

"I don't know! You know how I am. I open my mouth, and words fall out," I said. "I'm going to be more circumspect." Then, we both cackled, knowing that was unlikely.

But Jill was right. It didn't matter whether I liked my job. It didn't matter to Frank, or to Sean, or to Matt, one of the partners, or to anyone else at the company. The only thing that mattered was whether I was being productive, doing the tasks I'd been assigned to do, and doing them well. Frank had told I'd be judged on three things:

1. Volume
2. Quality
3. Efficiency

While there was a clear relationship between volume and efficiency, the interaction between volume and quality was more likely an inverse one. Surely, the greater the volume I produced, the more likely that quality was to suffer, but now I had an idea of the parameters I'd be judged on—similar to having billable hour requirements as a lawyer.

The question still remained, though, just how much volume? That was still murky. I was reminded of the Bible verse that says, "To whom much is given, much will be required," and suspected that what would be expected of me would be greater than what might be expected of a less experienced writer. I had started writing down what I did every day for several reasons:

1. To be able to set reasonable goals for myself, for Frank and for the company about what I could produce in terms of content outlines.
2. To be able to track my productivity and know what I should aim for if I was working from home.
3. To be able to quantify my value when it came to asking for a raise. I was the first content specialist hired at Digital Edge, which meant that my job didn't have a specific pay range. The position had originally paid $35,000 but Frank had been able to get the partners

to boost that to $45,000. I wanted to get that number higher—in the $60,000 range, if possible. I'd run the numbers, and I needed at least another $10,000 a year to make my life work.

With just two weeks of experience here, I'd already told Frank that while I liked working here (which I needed to stop saying), I wasn't satisfied with the salary and wanted more flexibility. That was the difference between being a new employee and a new employee of a certain age. It didn't even occur to me not to say what I wanted and what I expected. Did I like the fact that Frank appreciated me and thought I was doing a great job? Sure. But, money... Money counts. Money matters. I decided not to hold off until the end of the year to ask for a raise. I'd bring it up at six months, or possibly at four. The worst that could happen is that the company would say no. After all, every month that went by that I didn't make what I wanted to make, I was losing the opportunity to save more for retirement.

I'd sold my soul, as I'd said to Jill the night before, and sold it cheap—if not my actual soul, at least my physical body and presence, for just over $20/hour. But I wasn't feeling anxious. And I was learning a lot. I stroked myself with these thoughts the way you'd soothe a frightened kitten, and resolved to put my head down, work, and stop thinking about how ridiculously low my hourly rate was now when it used to average $100/hour as a freelancer. Pondering these kinds of thoughts at work was counterproductive—not to mention depressing.

I knew from my sporadic flirting with Buddhist ideas that emotions were impermanent. Any feeling I swam in at the moment wasn't an accurate reflection of how happy, or how unhappy, I was at work. Nor an indicator of how happy I might be in the future. An emotion is only a snapshot, like a blood pressure reading, not a comprehensive report; it shouldn't be taken as anything more than a moment in time.

I was still trying to run nearly every morning before work, with the end result of cutting it very close to getting to work on time. One morning I woke up late, but I still dashed to the Y, jumped on the treadmill, and clocked a four-mile run before hurrying home to take the world's shortest shower. On the way to work, I managed to hit every red light on the way and walked in a full five minutes late, already stressed out, only to discover that Frank wasn't there. He'd sent an email to let the content team know he was home, sick.

Well, thank you, universe. I settled in, caught up on my email, and discovered that a client was unhappy with the content I'd written last week. The AM reported that the client had said (among other things): "Sentences are often long and redundant. Content should be professional and easily 'digestible' by readers who have milliseconds to decide if they're interested in learning more. For example, 'ABC Company's product also saves additional money by eliminating the need for costlier reefers for shipping.' Why not just say, "ABC Company's product also helps cut costs by eliminating the need for reefers?"

Because of Google. We were to include at least 450 words of content for every page, which meant I was intentionally padding my writing. Forget writing "tight." Now my writing got fluffy—and fluffier.

Frank's note followed on the heels of the email from the account manager:

"This is a classic case of valuable feedback from a hands-on client at the outset of a campaign. This is how we learn and adjust to a client's preferences.

"Also, it goes to show that *some* clients do pay close attention to content production. Not all are as picky; some are pickier.

"After a cursory look, I didn't see any feedback that seemed unfair. If you think there is, let me know, and we can discuss how to proceed.

"Otherwise, don't take the feedback personally. This happens regularly with hands-on clients. We normally can make adjustments and match preferences."

My first reaction to the email about the client's dissatisfaction was a surge of anxiety. I'd screwed up! Then, my ego immediately stepped in. The client thought it was wordy? Well, that's what was going to happen when I wrote to word count—I often had to s-t-r-e-t-c-h the content to get to 450 words for word count. There were only so many attributes about the client's product and its benefits I could describe, so I was stuck adding words wherever I could. Wordy, padded, and yes, redundant content was the result. Fortunately, the AM had explained this to the client, who had agreed to lower the word count to a more reasonable figure—300 words per page, Google be damned. Now I was to rewrite the four pages I'd written, taking her feedback into account. I added the pages to my ever-present to-do list, mildly annoyed at the rewrites. No writer enjoys that.

But.

I wasn't going to make less money as a result. As a freelancer, rewrites meant that my hourly rate took a nosedive. As an employee, I was going to make the same amount of money regardless of whether each piece of content took one hour or five. It didn't matter. I was being paid to work eight hours a day, every day, which made it easier to shrug it off and rewrite the pages, eliminating about one-third of the words that were there, with the result being tighter, cleaner writing—the kind of work I'd do when I wasn't trying to reach an unrealistic word count. If one of the benchmarks I'd be measured on was quality, SEO was going to impair that.

That was another reason to continue freelancing—to help me maintain the quality of my work while boosting my income. Nancy's agent was shopping her book to publishers, and once it sold, I would find the time to write the book. I'd already put in eight months on the proposal and wanted to see the project through. The question was when I was actually going to do it.

In the morning, I was rushed from the time I woke up: getting up; dashing to the Y for my anxiety-easing run; getting home to shower, wake the kids and get ready for work before driving off; and then after work, every errand and chore—laundry, groceries, making dinner, cleaning the house, even running by the library—had to be performed in the gap between work and collapsing into bed. Yes, this is what single working parents did. And yes, I had been spoiled by freelancing, when I could incorporate all of these tasks, including socializing, into my day.

Adding to this pressure was the idea that I had to experience quality time with the kids every night since I wasn't spending as much time with them. To me, that meant a home-made, healthy dinner every night. We had to sit at the table. We had to put our phone away. There had to be conversation. Good conversation. Bonding.

So why did it seem impossible? I'd already bought healthy food to make for dinner, failed to cook it, and would up throwing it in the trash, which was expensive, maddening, and frustrating. One night, I heated up frozen beef and broccoli with Minute Rice for Ryan and made mac and cheese for Haley. I'd been eating packaged crap from the nook all afternoon and wasn't hungry, so I sipped a glass of wine while the two of them shoveled packaged crap food into their mouths. Haley insisted on sitting on the kitchen counter, and I let her. And we talked. And laughed. And I realized that it wasn't the actual food that mattered (though there did have to be some kind of food) but making time to unwind with them.

If weekday mornings and evenings were out, that left the weekends for Nancy's book, and I had grown to love my weekends. Two mornings to sleep in, without the rush of getting ready for work, and the expectation of two whole days stretching before me that were all mine — well, unless Ryan had a basketball tournament or Haley had a birthday party or a sleepover with a friend or some other activity that required parental transportation. I could count on seeing Walt at some point, who would drive over and meet me at one of Ryan's tourneys or show up in the afternoon. He and I would go to dinner or hang out and eat with the kids, and then spend Sundays lazing around, reading the paper, doing the crossword, and watching golf or football, depending on the season.

That Sunday night, our neighbors had had the four of us over for dinner, and we'd stayed several hours, talking and laughing while the kids played downstairs. After we came home, Walt left for the week, and Haley and I read together in my bed.

I looked over at her. "Why don't you sleep in here tonight?" I suggested.

She was thrilled. "Let me get my stuff." She dashed back into my bedroom with "Fluffy" (Fluffy Baby, a demented-looking baby doll with fading ink tattoos on her head) and "Pokey" (her polka-dot blanket, which she had had since birth.) She arranged herself on what I now thought of as Walt's side of the bed, and we talked and giggled until it was time for us to go to sleep.

I got up and said good night to Ryan, who was sprawled on his bed, looking at his phone, came back and climbed into bed with Haley. I leaned over and kissed her. "I love you," I said. "A tiny, tiny bit."

She giggled. I never said I loved my kids to the moon and back or any such exaggeration even if it was true. Instead, I always said I loved them a tiny bit, which still made Haley laugh.

The next morning, I crept out of bed, careful not to wake Haley, and started my usual weekday routine, rebooted from the weekend. That feeling might only last a few hours once I arrived at work, but I was grateful for every two-day respite.

At work, though, there was little to ease the occasional boredom I felt. I wound up snacking on the nearly inexhaustible supply of packaged crap in the nook when I was hungry, simply looking for something to do, or had reached that I-don't-give-a-crap stage of the day where my willpower was gone and my desire for instant gratification was overwhelming.

I'd gained a few pounds since I'd started the job. I knew what I needed to do— tune into my body, feed it when it was hungry, and stop using food as a reward or for anything other than energy and fuel. Most of the time, I didn't obsess over my weight. I'd accepted that my body would never be the slim, sculpted ideal I'd spent much of my teens and twenties striving (and failing) to achieve and that my physical imperfections, while numerous, were mostly concealed under my clothes. Yet, when I felt fat, and there were plenty of times when I did, I also felt gross and disgusting. (I never felt fat without also feeling gross, and disgusting. Those emotional states remained entangled, even at 52, when I should have known better.)

The speed at which the packaged crap disappeared from the nook meant I wasn't the only person at work falling victim to fatty and salty snacks, but I also wasn't a 20-something whose body simply absorbed the excess calories and moved on. Most days, I felt 25, but my physical body was not.

A Midlife Woman's List of Ways You Know You're 52, Not 25 (Even If You Say You Still *Feel* 25)

1. A sleepless night destroys you the next day. You're not simply tired. You are barely able to function.
2. You wake up with random pains that have no identifiable cause. You can become injured by a night of sleep or simply reaching for your keys.
3. You lose all enthusiasm for dieting. I knew I should do something about my meno-pot, but I couldn't muster the drive to actually do something or even anything about it (like cut back on carbs, count calories or go on an actual diet) other than wear control-top tights and bemoan it to my friend Hannelore while we drank wine and ate salty snacks and cookies. I could no longer starve myself in an attempt to lose weight. I couldn't even manage to be hungry for any length of time. I might drop dead tomorrow, I'd tell myself. And if I do drop dead tomorrow, I wouldn't want to have spent the day before hungry, cranky, and listless.
4. You now exercise, not for vanity's sake or to train for a race but to relieve stress, to avoid gaining any more weight (you hope), and, hopefully, to reduce your risk of heart disease, diabetes, cancer, you name it. You lift weights because you fear osteoporosis. You can still run (at a slower pace than ever before) but recognize that speed walking around your neighborhood is not far off in your future.
5. You worry more than you ever did before. At 25, my biggest concerns were billing enough hours every week

as a lawyer; stretching my paycheck to pay for my car, my rent, my student loans, and, oh, yeah, food; and worrying whether I'd be able to run eight miles without stopping for the first time with my marathon training group. (I could!) Now I was responsible for two actual human beings (and a demanding, entitled cat), and I had to be able to make enough money to support the three of us, save for retirement, save for their college, pay for their orthodontia (because each of them needs a full set of braces), and hope that I was parenting them with enough thoughtfulness, compassion, and practicality that they will both turn into self-sufficient, emotionally well-adjusted, self-supporting, decent human beings—and that's not even touching on whether your mother's occasional forgetfulness is normal age-related behavior or something you need to become even more worried about, terror attacks, global warming, macular degeneration, the current president, the economy, or the fact that you still haven't had that colonoscopy …

I, of course, kept these worries to myself. I was still working on getting everyone's names down, using the floor plan of the office that had people's names, but every day or so I came across yet another employee I didn't recognize. I now knew all of the SEO guys, the sales guys, the handful of project managers who sat on the other side of the office, and the PPC team, even if the latter all sat at their desks with headsets on and rarely seemed to speak.

The rest of the departments— creative, development, and content marketing—were still mysteries to me. I'd introduced myself to nearly everyone I encountered in the nook or in the bathroom, but I'd been there for two months. How long could I keep saying, "Good morning! I'm Kelly. I'm new here. I don't think I've met you yet?" So, I simply nodded or said, "Good morning," and went about my day.

I had expected more of a team atmosphere, but the only people I interacted with regularly were the sales guys. They were the extroverts in a company full of geeks, and they joked, bantered, and laughed with each other all day, swapping strategy and good-natured insults, often about each other's golf prowess (or lack of it). I soaked that up, feeling absurdly flattered if they included me in conversation.

Marcus, the vice president of sales, sat with the rest of his team, a group of guys in their late 20s to mid-30s. Marcus was a Renaissance man, who knew a little about just about everything, whether you were talking about the origins of rap music to trickle-down economics to politics to sports. He was smart, confident and had boundless energy. I knew from creeping his LinkedIn page that he had founded his own company which had then been acquired by Digital Edge, and while he still wore that entrepreneurial spirit, he was also a team-builder by nature, greeting all of his team when he strode in every morning—unlike the way most people slid into their cubicles without even saying hello, as if they didn't want anyone to notice they had arrived. On his way out, Marcus fist-bumped his guys good-bye. I liked his energy and was absorbing a lot about how SEO campaigns worked simply by virtue of where I sat.

Marcus also swore with impunity, and I'd witnessed him lose his temper more than once. "Mother fucker!" he yelled one afternoon while trying to load a deck, or presentation, before a potential call. "This fucking deck! What the fuck! This piece of fucking shit!" It went on like that for a few minutes as he banged his keyboard in increasing frustration. I kept my head down, but I appreciated the demonstration that we were, in fact, human beings, prone to anger and frustration, not simply mindless headphone-wearing cogs who churned out work for eight hours every Monday through Friday.

Melissa had been working for DE for a couple of weeks and had picked up the job quickly—more quickly than I'd expected. She was quiet, but I appreciated having someone to talk to, even sporadically, throughout the day. I might ask Frank an occasional question, but most of our communication was done via email. The editors, Evie and Sarah, both seemed nice, but neither was particularly outgoing. Roger was always head-down, absorbed in his work. I felt like I was pestering him when I had to ask a question, so I tried to handle any issues on my own even though Workfront still flummoxed me.

Often, I had questions about a particular client, such as whether the keywords had been approved or whether a particular keyword could be swapped out with something else to make for easier writing. Instead of emailing, I'd walk over and pester the SEO guys, who sat in a row across from Sean and a couple of other tech guys whose roles I still hadn't confirmed. I'd walk over with a notebook and pen, my questions at the ready. "Okay, gentlemen! Good morning!" I'd say. "Who has ABC Company? I've got a question for you!"

"That's me," Kevin or Seth or one of the other guys would say, turning in his chair. "What's up?"

I had no problems asking questions. I had 20 or 30 years on these guys, but I was always willing to admit when I didn't know the answer to a question. I also wanted to know the "why." When we were told to write a meta description for every piece of content, I wanted to know why. What exactly was the purpose of a meta description? Why did it have to be 155 characters? Why did it have to include a call to action? Was there a difference between a singular keyword and a plural keyword? Why could e-com pages include just 100 words but landing pages needed 450?

Before I'd started working with the SEO team, I'd asked Frank a lot of these questions; he had either answered them or sent me to Sean. I'd belatedly realized that Sean wasn't just a random techie but the director of Internet services, which meant he was higher on the food chain than Frank and, in fact, higher on the food chain than anyone other than the partners themselves.

I'd been kicking an idea around about how to streamline the content team's process for handling optimization pages but needed more information to make the case for it. We had three options for onsite content: you created a new page ("create"), optimized the current content without adding anything new ("optimize"), or expanded existing content to include keywords, adding enough words to make Google pay attention ("expand"). One morning, I stopped by Sean's desk.

"Hey, Sean, do you have a second? And good morning!"

"Sure. What's up?"

"For onsite content, we have three options—create, optimize or expand. So, how does that work for clients? Do we charge more for a new page versus an optimization page?"

He paused. "What do you mean?"

"I'm just wondering if we charge clients more for new or expansion pages over optimization pages because the former are more work. If I were the client and saw I was paying the same amount for optimization pages, which aren't that much work, I'd wonder why I was paying more for something that doesn't take that much time," I continued. "So, are there different rates?"

"No." He shook his head. "They're all the same."

I nodded. "Okay. So how much do we charge for a page?"

He spoke slowly. "It doesn't work like that. The client's

campaign determines what work we do for it: how many backlinks, onsite pages, and/or content assets we're going to do. But we don't break it down like that."

"Still, though, you must have an idea of what the value of each page is."

He shook his head. "We don't break it down like that."

But why don't you, I almost asked, but realized I wasn't going to get an answer. Instead, I thanked him and walked back to my desk. I'd worked for content agencies before and knew that they charged clients based on the amount of work created, so there had to be some figure attached to a page of content. I knew from talking with Frank that we paid freelancers between $50 and $120 or so for a page of content, so what the client was billed had to be significantly higher than that. That's how business worked. Was a page worth $200? $300? More? Less? I knew that clients paid as little as $500/month for an SEO campaign that included a technical audit, identifying and cleaning up backlinks, creating higher quality backlinks, and other technical aspects of SEO, like making sure webpages had appropriate title tags and metatags in addition to the actual content we created, expanded, or optimized.

I decided to shrug it off and proceed with my idea, asking to meet Frank in Yahoo a few days later, the first time I'd been the one to initiate a meeting. It stemmed from our team's usual process for creating onsite content:

1. The SEO analyst notified Melissa and me through Workfront that target pages and keywords had been approved by the client.
2. Melissa or I created the outline for each target page in one of our two Excel spreadsheets (A-M and N-Z), notifying Roger when they were completed.

3. Roger used the outline to create a complete assignment for the writer, updated the task on Workfront, and forwarded the assignment to Frank.

4. Frank assigned the piece to a staff or freelance writer. Currently, there were two DE writers: Dave, who worked full time, from home, and Penny, who worked part time from home. The rest of the writing was sent to freelancers whom Frank managed.

5. The writer turned the piece in to Frank, who assigned it to Evie or Sarah to be edited.

6. After editing, the piece was saved in the relevant folder on the company server, and the AM was notified.

7. The AM then forwarded it to the client for approval; once the client approved, it was implemented. If the client requested revisions, it came back to Frank, who would then reassign it for a rewrite.

It was a lot of steps for each piece of content. What if we could keep some of these target pages out of the funnel? What if Melissa and I kept a running list of what we called "rework" pages (because we'd be reworking the content to incorporate keywords), and optimized them when we had time, instead of sending them through the regular process? We wouldn't have to write outlines for them, Roger and Frank wouldn't have process them, and they wouldn't have to be assigned out to writers.

I explained my idea to Frank. "The optimization pages don't take long at all," I said. "It seems like a waste of time to handle them the same way as new pages and expansion pages. We'd all save time, and you wouldn't have to assign them out. What do you think?"

Frank thought about it for a minute. "Are you sure you'd have time?"

"Yes," I said eagerly. "There are plenty of times when we are slow on outlines. Besides, sometimes it's nice to have a break from outlines. And that would mean we wouldn't have to send out so many pieces of content to freelancers, which would save the department money." I knew from asking that he paid freelancers between $50 and $120 for one piece of content, and that was the rate the agency charged. The writers themselves made less than that, which meant they were making less than $0.10/word.

"Let me think about it," he said. "But it sounds like it might work."

I told Frank about my recent conversation with Sean and that I was surprised that DE didn't have a set value on each piece of content. He nodded, arms crossed over his chest as usual. "He mentioned you've been asking a lot of questions," he said. It was clear that Sean hadn't meant it in a complimentary way.

"He did?" I sighed, deflated. "Well, you have told me more than once to ask him. Besides, I thought asking questions was a good thing."

"You have to understand that most people here don't ask questions," said Frank. "They come to work, do their jobs, and go home."

I shook my head, ignoring his point. "That makes no sense to me," I said. "I'm trying to figure out how all the pieces fit together here. The more I know, the better able I am to do my job." I was going to keep asking questions. I'd just have to be more selective about whom I asked.

As my knowledge grew, I continued to track my production numbers, evidence (I hoped) of my value. My plan was to quantify what I brought to the company. If I could point to how much I'd produced for the company or how many dollars

I'd saved, I'd have a better chance of getting a raise—not just a raise, but a sizeable one.

If Frank was right, most of my coworkers did whatever their job descriptions entailed, whether that was building backlinks, editing content, analyzing target pages, or uploading content. I couldn't do that. I had run a business fairly successfully for years and the reason had to do less with the kind of writing I provided (straightforward, service-oriented, conversational) and more to do with the kind of writer I was (easy to work with, flexible, reliable). I had had to be willing to learn about new subjects and tackle different types of assignments. I had grown, adapted, learned, and built my career around three words: mindset, efficiency, connections.

Mindset meant treating my writing like a business. It meant setting goals for myself, whether that was my daily nut or replying to a rejection from an editor with a new idea or pitch within 24 hours (my 24-hour rule). It meant that I considered the LTP, or long-term potential, of any new project or client. I wasn't looking for one-off assignments but clients and publications that would become regulars.

Efficiency meant that I worked for the same clients as often as I could because they were more likely to say yes to pitches. In many cases, my editors came to me with assignments, which meant I didn't have to pitch; every freelancer knows that pitching is a necessary but time-consuming part of the business. I specialized in health, fitness, and nutrition and tended to write about the same subjects more than once to maximize my research time. I focused on service-oriented articles and books because they took less time to produce than other types of writing, like essays or narrative nonfiction.

The connections piece? I had grown my business by creating relationships with the people I worked with, whether they were editors or clients or sources or other writers. I employed the golden rule whenever I could and found that I thrived in an introvert's business because I liked connecting with people and valued relationships.

I'd thought I could apply similar strategies at a job, but the connections piece was a challenge. I had yet to make a real friend at work though Melissa was a strong contender. She and I talked throughout the day, and I'd occasionally call a meeting in Yahoo for the two of us just because I could. We'd go over a few work items and then sit and gossip a bit though there wasn't much to gossip about. Mostly we commiserated over challenging clients and tricky keywords, but I did my best to mentor her, trying to help her navigate the strange world of Digital Edge.

When the company migrated the remaining 50 or so Digital Plus clients over, Melissa and I would be responsible for outline creation for 150 clients, plus whatever writing tasks Frank assigned. A team of two could certainly do more work than one, but that fact created a new worry. Melissa was a year out of college and capable of doing the job I'd been hired to do, at (I was certain) a significantly lower salary. Did that mean my job was less secure? My 20 years of experience might not mean anything when a 23-year-old could do my job. Why couldn't the company keep her, after I'd trained her, then fire me, and save money in the long run?

I'd never had these worries before. As a freelancer, I'd built my business on relationships. Editors and clients knew that I'd turn in my work on time, that I'd fulfill the specs of the assignment, and that I would complete any revisions without complaint. Here I was a proverbial cog, and a minor cog at that, in a wheel that could be swapped with another cog at any time.

I had little time to ponder this on February 27, when a crisis erupted. Our client, which sold spring break trips to high school and college students, had a dozen pages of content due at month's end, but somewhere along the line, the pages had failed to be assigned out. That meant we had two days to write and edit the pages before submitting them to the AM. We didn't have time to create outlines; instead, Frank simply assigned eight pages to me and four to Melissa. Each page had minimal existing content and had to be expanded to 450 words each, while incorporating the relevant keywords, which we highlighted in yellow to make them stand out.

I had other work, too. While Melissa and I were caught up on outlines (at least until we got keyword approval on the next batch of clients), I had several other rush assignments for a high-end travel company that were also due the next day. I'd have to shoehorn the new rush pages alongside the earlier rushes.

The diversity of clients we worked for meant that I was constantly changing mental hats. On any given day, I might be writing about passive temperature protection products, family engagement software for schools, custom chemical manufacturing, personal injury law, and boudoir photography—all in the same morning.

That afternoon I flipped between the spring break company and the other client, a travel firm that specialized in high-end nature cruises for well-heeled travelers who wanted to tick the North Pole and other destinations off their bucket lists. I had an easier time channeling my wealthy inner snob than my inner Millennial (and had to resort to Googling "slang Millennials use" to try to write the copy for the spring break company). I was forced to ask 24-year-old Melissa questions like, "Do Millennials still say 'FOMO'?" ("Um, no," she replied.) I hadn't even realized a portion of my audience was Generation Z, a generation I actually should know something about since I was mother to two of its members.

I tried. I wrote:

When you hear Panama City Beach spring break, do you say hell, yeah? You should. A Panama City spring break will be like nothing you've experienced before. So, leave the cold weather, classes and boredom behind as you head down for the party of a lifetime. Don't fall victim to FOMO. Show up ready to make this trip one that you and the rest of your squad will never forget. (Yes, I used FOMO after all! And squad!)

Five minutes later, I was writing:

The British Isles. Few places are as rich in history and beauty as Great Britain. From the hushed reverence of a Benedictine abbey to the cacophony of dozens of species of birds on uninhabited Irish islands to geological masterpieces that appear to have been hewn by giants, you'll have no shortage of once-in-a-lifetime memories on this trip. Your senses will come alive as you explore parts of the world where time seems to have stood still—while experiencing a powerful pull to the past. The onboard amenities and the wealth of sensory experiences you have off the ship will ensure that this is a trip like none other. One that you'll savor not only during your cruise but in the weeks and months to come thereafter.

The hushed reverence of a Benedictine abbey? Where did I even come up with this stuff? Who cared? My brain had been engaged, and I had welcomed the challenge, even while writing for two radically different clients in the space of an hour made me feel bipolar (North Pole pun intended). Melissa and I worked steadily, turning in pieces of content to be edited as soon as we completed each one.

At the end of the next day, Frank praised Melissa and me for our ability to churn out these pieces in time for them to be edited before the end of day on February 28—and make the deadline. "Sean's happy," he said. "I think he sees the value in having people on the team who can jump in and write like that."

It might have been a small thing, but it made me feel good. And valued. And noticed.

I told the kids about my minor work victory when they came home from Erik's that Sunday afternoon. I made spaghetti with vegetarian meatballs, and we sat and talked. I'd been irritable with both of them lately and apologized for it. "I feel like I haven't been that great of a parent lately," I admitted. "I want to do better. What kinds of things would you like to do more of with me? How do you want to spend your time at night when I get home? Like what would you like to do after dinner?"

(Side note: welcome to parenting today. Did my mom, dad, or stepdad, ask, even one time, how he or she could "do better?" Nope. Yet, I had been culturally conditioned, and now I continually felt guilty/selfish/lax/subpar/you name it by my sometimes-lackluster parenting.)

Ryan shrugged. He was mastering the teenage boy's shrug—one part indifference, one part insolence, one part cockiness. I mentally rolled my eyes and turned to my daughter.

"I want to go the Y more," Haley said. "And run on the track."

I wasn't surprised. She loved to put on my headphones and run. That was an easy ask. Except it was challenging enough to get to the Y first thing in the morning, before work, when I was fresh and had not yet been beaten down by the day. Now, I was supposed to go there after work as well?

"Okay," I said. We can do that more." (As with so many things parenting-related, you agree to something and hope that you'll never have to actually do it.) But Haley never forgot anything, especially something that benefited her. The next night, it was on. "But you promised," she said, while I sat with my feet up on the couch after dinner. I caved, and she ran on the track, listening to music on my iPhone, while I sat in the lobby, read a book, and patted myself on the back for being a parent who kept her promises.

The Corporate Newbie's Cheat Sheet: Balancing Your Job with the Rest of Your Life

This is an easy one. Work/life balance doesn't exist, so forget about achieving it.

I'm kidding. (Kind of.) But the fact is that I know literally no woman, especially one with kids at home, who claims that she has achieved work/life balance. Errands get forgotten. Workouts get skipped. Kids get yelled at. And shit doesn't get done.

My radical idea? Forget about work/life balance, and instead, focus on one or two absolutes. For me, this is working out in the morning before work, at least three mornings a week. Yes, it means I have to get up earlier and burn time driving to and from the gym in addition to my run, but I feel so much better afterwards, and, I believe, am more productive, too.

My only other absolute is that the kids and I eat dinner together, every night, unless an event like basketball practice makes that impossible. When I started this job, I also committed to cooking dinner for the three of us. My reasoning was sound, but I ignored the fact that I don't enjoy cooking. It is one of the last things I want to do at the end of a workday. No, takeout Chinese, Kraft mac and cheese, and takeout pizza aren't as healthy as a homecooked meal, but it is food—and we do still sit together, for at least a few minutes, and connect.

So, my advice is to choose several must-haves, and let some of that other stuff slide, especially during your first few weeks on your new job. You're undergoing a tremendous amount of stress between learning new software, trying to get everyone's names down, figuring out what's expected of you in terms of work, and performing as best as you can at your new career. If that means you rely on takeout food for a few weeks, your kids won't suffer, and you won't, either. I also made it easy for myself by grouping the five or six work dresses I have in the closet. In the morning, I don't think about what I'm going to wear. I just grab the next dress in the rotation. When I get home, I take it off, shake it out if it's still clean (it usually is), and hang it back up. If it's dirty or needs washing or dry cleaning, I throw it in the wash.

Finally, accept that you're getting into a new groove, and that's going to feel awkward and uncomfortable, at least for a while. But when you know what your must-haves are, you can focus on meeting them and let some of the other shit slide.

CHAPTER 5

Deliverables

The next week, Frank emailed me, asking me to sit in on a phone conference between Heidi, an AM, and a client. The client wasn't happy with we'd produced for its site, and Frank wanted me on the call to represent the content team and to see if I could glean any insights into what the client was looking for.

I didn't want to be on the call. What did I have to offer? I was an underling, hired to populate spreadsheets with phrases like "please create content for a new page…" That feeling vanished once the call started, and the client, the VP of the company, expressed concern about the overall tone of the pages.

"We feel like the content isn't talking to our customers," said the vice president. "We want it to be more you-oriented."

Wait a minute! This was my bailiwick. I could speak her language.

"Heidi, can I jump in here?" I asked.

When Heidi consented, I stepped into the gap as neatly as if I'd been doing it for years. (Wait a minute! I had.) I had already skimmed the website and the content we'd written ahead of the call.

"I agree," I said. "It's talking too much about your company and what you offer and not enough about the benefits to your customers. It needs to be more customer focused."

"Exactly," said the VP. "And it's overwritten. Wordy."

"That may be due in part to SEO," I said. "Sometimes, we have to expand the content to get up to a certain number of words—say, 450 —for Google, and that can result in content that feels wordy." What I called padded. "But I understand your concerns, and we can certainly take a closer look at it and make it more concise."

The VP and I spoke a bit longer.

"Anything else we should be aware of?"

"Oh! I should have said this before. Our CEO is a stickler for contractions. He doesn't like them or want to use them on the website."

That meant the language was going to sound a little stiff and formal, but if that was what the client wanted, that was what the client would get. "'Do not use contractions,'" I repeated. "I'll make a note of that going forward."

I shared my notes with Frank afterward, passing along the client's feedback. A few minutes later, I received an email from Heidi. The subject line read, "Shout-out to Kelly James," and she thanked and complimented me for building trust with the client, ending with "great to have you on the team." She had cc'd her boss and Frank on it, which I appreciated. I left work that day feeling smart and valued. And possibly even valuable.

I was starting to realize that most of our clients didn't understand SEO or how it worked. I barely had a toehold myself. An SEO campaign took time to take root. It was like turning an ocean liner; it took a long time to execute the turn, and you likely didn't feel it even as it happened. But our clients could read. If they paid more attention to the changes and/ or additions we were making to their websites, they might be more patient with results or grasp that those changes represented progress even before their sites started to crawl up the Google rankings, a process which took months.

I explained my reasoning to Frank the next day and suggested having a content team member (you know, like me) on the kickoff calls, when he was standing by my desk.

"We can't do that," was his response.

"Who says we can't?" I answered.

"I don't have 20 writers sitting around to do that."

"We don't need 20 writers," I said. "We could have a content team member on the bigger accounts. Plus, we could ask if there are any content issues we should be aware of when creating the content. It might be something as small as ABC Company not liking contractions, but that's the kind of info that could save us time and mean fewer rewrites. Plus, the client would hopefully feel listened to in terms of content." I doubled down on my argument, but Frank shook his head and walked away.

A savvier person would have moved on. But I was confident that my idea was a good one, and yes, evidence of my value. So, I stopped by Matt's office a few mornings later. He was one of the four partners, and the only one I'd actually spoken with before.

I tapped on his door. "Good morning, Matt," I said. "Do you have a couple of minutes? I'd like to run something by you."

Matt nodded, and I sat down. I explained about my idea to keep optimization pages in-house. Frank had okayed it, and Melissa and I now kept a running list of these pages, optimizing them in between writing outlines. "It makes the process more efficient on our end, and we don't have to send those pages out to freelancers, so it saves the department money, too," I explained.

I segued into my idea of having a content person on the kickoff call, at least for major clients. "There seems to be a disconnect sometimes between what clients expect and what we deliver," I said. "Having someone from the content team on the call could give us more insight into what the client is looking for and help the client understand what is going to happen, content-wise. I ran this by Frank, and he said he doesn't have writers sitting around to be able to do this, but it seems like something worth considering."

Matt listened. "Our focus right now is getting Digital Plus up and running, and I love that you're looking for ways to make the process more efficient and effective," he said. "I'll definitely think about this idea. It might be something to consider going forward."

He stood up, coffee cup in hand, and I recognized my cue to leave. I sashayed my way down the hallway, feeling like I was in it to win it. I was a baller! Look at me, slaying corporate America. The adrenaline high lasted most of the morning, even when I realized that Melissa and I were caught up on outlines. All I had to do was a couple of writing assignments for Frank, neither of which would take very long.

I worked on them with no particular urgency, caught up on email, wasted time for a while, reading my favorite website, Dlisted, a scathing gossip site that was both snarky and well-written, and watched the clock. If I were freelancing, I would have knocked off for the day, but I still had a couple of hours to sit in my chair and be paid.

A bit later, Frank stopped by my desk. "I've got something for you."

"Sure, boss. What's up?"

Frank told me he wanted me to rewrite a piece of content for a new client, a high-end architectural company that specialized in four-star resort design. "Their feedback on the first page was horrible," he said.

"The feedback was horrible, or the feedback was that the first page was horrible?" I asked.

"Both. I'd like you to take a stab at it."

I'd created the outlines for the client, so I'd seen its website. It was eye-popping, clean, and its content read like Architectural Digest. "I can," I said. "And I'm happy to do so, but I have to say my sense is that the client is going to be hard to please."

I reviewed the page our writer had produced. I was surprised at how good it was. I'd describe much of the content that Digital Edge produced as serviceable but nothing special. SEO drove the content, not style, voice, or originality. The bar was set low: follow the outline, make sure you got the keywords in, move on. As a freelancer, I'd prided myself on the quality of my work. I might be writing service journalism, but I took the time to toy with the lead of a story until its cadence resonated, to choose my language with precision, and to close a piece with a kicker that related back to the lead. I didn't turn in a piece until I was pleased with its quality.

Now, I usually had a day, maybe two, to write a piece and the process was different. As a freelancer, my background research and interviews dictated my approach to a story. After interviewing sources, whether experts or "real people" for anecdotes, I'd reach through my transcripts for the most compelling quotes and use them to frame the story. Typically, I had at least a week or two, if not longer, to research and write a piece. That time give me the opportunity to think about a piece, to play with a draft, and to edit, rewrite, tinker, and polish until I was happy with my work.

I didn't tinker much with my writing for DE. I'd read through the outline, check the GCI (general client information) document for any specific client notes, review the provided resources, and then follow the outline. I had little latitude in terms of approach; I simply had to write at least 450 words, incorporating keywords. Or I'd expand an existing page by another 100 or 200 words, including keywords. Or I'd rework the piece to include keywords, making minor edits so that I wasn't shoehorning them in.

I'd already made a division in my mind between the work I did as a freelancer and the work I did for DE. One was writing. One was creating content. The former felt like craft. The latter felt much of the time like making widgets, but that's what I was being paid to do for 42.5 hours every week, with my butt in my chair at the office.

But did my butt have to be at the office? I'd asked Frank the week before if I could work from home on a Thursday. Haley had a performance at school—the third- and fourth-grade classes were singing "folk songs, work songs, and sea shanties," whatever the latter was.

"Can you come, Mom? Please?"

Truth be told, I didn't really care if I saw her perform or not. There's always another event coming up, another soccer game, another basketball tourney, another something. Yes, I know that time only moves in one direction and that the number of these events is finite, but sometimes I don't want to have to go.

"Of course."

I approached the topic with Frank the next day in the nook. "Frank, if I want to work from home, do you have to know why? Or may I just ask to work from home?"

He thought about a minute. "I don't have to know why," he said.

"All right. Well, I am going to tell you in this case," I said. "Haley has a performance at school I don't want to miss." I emailed him next, reminding him, and he agreed to let me work from home that morning. I ran at the Y, showered and dressed, but instead of rushing to slip on a wrap dress, I snuggled into my overalls, which I hadn't worn in weeks.

I settled into my usual Command Central position on the couch, emailing Frank a few minutes before 8:00 a.m. so he'd know he was at my "desk."

By the time I drove to Haley's school, the gym was already packed with the less-neglectful parents who had arrived earlier than I to secure prime video positions. Erik was sitting on the stage, and I squeezed in beside him. As I sat down, I scanned the dozens of kids sitting on the bleachers. Haley was craning her neck, looking around, and when she saw me, her face burst open with joy. "Mommy!" She waved her arm frantically at me.

I waved back, swallowing the rush of emotion I felt. And I hadn't wanted to come! I sat, watched, listened, applauded the kids, and waved at her when she walked out, head high, a huge smile on her face. I picked her up from after-school care a little after 4:30. "I was so proud of you today," I told her. "You nailed your speaking part."

She grinned, and she chattered happily on the way home. When I put her to bed, I kissed her good night. "I'm so glad I got to see you sing today," I told her. "I'll be sure to ask my boss to work from home for anything else you have during school, okay?"

"Good." She snuggled down under her blankets with Fluffy and Pokey in her arms.

I made a point of thanking Frank for letting me work from home the next morning. He had asked to meet with me in Google to talk about Melissa's progress; Yahoo was booked.

"She's doing great," I said. "And she's not afraid to ask questions if she's not sure about something." He asked what I thought of her writing, and I was honest.

"Sometimes, she uses the wrong word," I said. "Or her writing is a little too flowery for a landing page, but overall, her writing is solid." Definitely good enough for Digital Edge,

I thought but didn't say. Frank bristled when any kind of criticism, even constructive, was offered about the company. I brought up the revision I'd done for the for the high-end architect client, but he hadn't heard back from the AM about it yet. That wasn't unusual; while we had tight deadlines for content, it was sometimes weeks or even longer to hear back from clients on content.

"My understanding is that I was hired to do outlines," I said. "I'm always happy to take on whatever you need me to do, but the more tasks like this I have, the more it may affect my total numbers at the end of the month."

Frank stopped me. "How many DP clients that have keywords approved have we not done outlines for?"

I thought about it. "Well, zero, actually."

"Exactly. So, there's no problem."

"But don't my numbers matter?"

"Not if you're getting the work done."

"But I like tracking what I'm doing," I said. "How else am I supposed to measure my progress?"

"Isn't tracking your numbers putting pressure on you?" Frank countered.

"I guess …"

"That pressure is internal pressure," he said. "It's coming from you. I'm not asking for those numbers, am I?"

"Okay. I hear what you're saying," I said. "But I like having a certain level of productivity."

"Again, that's self-imposed pressure. I'm not asking what you're doing every day. You're getting your work done, and you have the freedom to determine how you spend your time. That makes your job different than a lot of other people here. If you're not up to something really taxing, you can choose something that isn't as demanding. It's up to you to determine how you spend your workday."

"I know, and I appreciate that." And then, emboldened by his trust in me, I told him about my recent conversation with Matt and that I had mentioned my idea of having someone from the content team (you know, like me) on calls with important, high-dollar clients.

Frank's face twitched. He was sitting with one leg crossed over his knee and his foot started jiggling faster and faster. As I watched his foot, it slowly dawned that I had overstepped.

"I'm sorry," I said, apologizing without meaning to. "I guess I'm trying to prove my value here," I offered. Before I could explain my thought process, he interrupted.

"Have I done anything or said anything to make you feel like you're not valuable?" asked Frank. "Have I ever indicated that I don't appreciate you?"

"Well, no ..." Had I missed something? Were we dating? This conversation sounded more romantic in nature than that of boss and subordinate. "I like having parameters. I like keeping track of things. It gives me a sense of accomplishment. And I'm still freelancing and working," I continued. My mouth was still in gear while my brain lagged behind. "I don't want to freelance anymore, but I have to because of what I'm making."

It had fallen out of my mouth, but there it was. I didn't want to freelance anymore. At least, I didn't want to freelance on top of working. It was too much. I had had one 400-word article to write for one of my favorite clients that week. The background research had taken maybe 20 minutes; lining up and conducting the interview, another 30, tops. I'd started pulling the piece together and needed maybe an hour of focused work to write it and get it done.

And I couldn't do it. I'd put it off Tuesday, Wednesday, and Thursday. Now it was Friday, and it was due Monday, which meant I was going to have to write it this weekend. Although the thought made me stabby, it was a $600 assignment, and I couldn't walk away from that money. I did want to keep my hand in … didn't I?

"It's only been two months," said Frank. "We'll revisit this in four months—that's six months before we normally do that. Then you can give me all of your numbers, and we'll go from there."

"Okay."

Frank's arms were still folded across his chest, and he still looked pissed. I bit off the urge to apologize yet again and resolved to move on, but Frank wasn't finished.

"You haven't been here that long," he reminded me. "You should realize that oftentimes a suggestion can come off as criticism."

I started to simmer. "But the partners said at the quarterly meeting that they want our feedback. They welcome ideas. They have an open-door policy," I parroted. My voice was starting to rise.

"That's true of some people here, yes. But others take that kind of feedback as criticism, especially when it doesn't have anything to do with your position."

Oh. Okay, then. I took a breath. "So … you're basically telling me to stay in my lane?"

"Exactly." His posture relaxed, just slightly.

I nodded. "Understood. I'll keep that in mind going forward."

He had told me to make the job my own. To run with it. As long as I didn't run too fast or too far. Or ask too many questions. Or offer too many ideas.

As a freelancer, I'd constantly challenged myself, looking for new markets, new clients, and new kinds of work. I'd started out writing for magazines and then branched out into books. I'd taught writing classes, spoken at writers' conference, and keynoted events. I'd launched a writer's newsletter, founded and written a popular blog for freelancers, and even written and sold a couple of "chick lit" novels before changing gears to focus primarily on ghostwriting books with some articles thrown in. None of this would have happened had I stayed in my lane.

I'd always thought that anyone could be a corporate wage worker, but not everyone could succeed as a freelancer. Not everyone could be a ghostwriter. I got paid to learn about a variety of subjects, talk to interesting people, and create pieces of writing that had not existed before. Pieces of writing that occasionally might even help someone, or entertain someone, or maybe encourage someone to make a positive change in his or her life. That mattered.

As a freelancer, I'd hit the six-figure mark one year and come close in others. I'd had freedom and flexibility when my kids were little. I'd enjoyed long lunches with girlfriends and spent lazy afternoons at the pool with the kids during summers. I'd been able to work from home, wear overalls, and have long conversations with people of all stripes for years at Peet's. I'd loved a lot of it, not the least part of which was succeeding at something that most people couldn't do.

But as time had passed, the good had started to be shadowed by the not-so-great and the downright unmanageable. That anxiety that I had sometimes mislabeled as energy and motivation had become more difficult to harness as I got older. The idea of sitting at my desk for 40 hours a week until the day I dropped wasn't exactly uplifting, but it was better than sitting on my couch with not enough work. I had chosen to transition to a real job, and eventually I wanted to be making enough that I no longer had to freelance. If I no longer had to, did I even want to?

If the answer was no, it wasn't worthwhile to go to ASJA, the writers' conference I attended in Manhattan every year. I'd been a member of the American Society of Journalists and Authors, an organization for full-time freelance journalists, for nearly 20 years. I'd joined as a relatively inexperienced writer and had found my tribe. Freelancers were, on the whole, smart, curious, talkative people who could converse about nearly any subject. They were independent, driven, and willing to take on the challenge of being self-employed. They understood not only the stress of taking on a challenging topic on a demanding deadline but the satisfaction as well. Over the years, I'd made dozens of writing buddies with whom I could talk, laugh, and commiserate. I had a core group of friends to whom I could reach out at any time to talk about a contract issue or a tricky story or just to complain about sources who went AWOL, ridiculous edit requests, clients who were snail-like in paying.

I'd booked my trip last December and had agreed to moderate a panel on ghostwriting, featuring agents (including my agent, Katherine) and editors. But why spend money (and PTO, of which I had precious little) to go to New York and burn hundreds of dollars … for what? I wasn't looking to meet new potential clients or sign a new book deal.

I debated reneging and finding someone to take over my panel. I asked the universe for a sign. Later that day, during a rare scroll through Instagram, I saw an Instagram post from Carolyn, a friend of mine through ASJA:

> When I first attended this conference just four years ago, I was nervous and felt so behind and out of place. I was a 20-something walking the halls with top editors and freelancers, and I felt like I knew no one and could never break into this elite world. But then I met @ healthbookghost and @ketteljm and a dozen other

fabulous women who took me under their wing and made me feel at home. I realized this was what it really meant to find my "tribe" in a profession where I'm often working at home alone.

@healthbookghost. That was me. I remembered meeting Carolyn. We'd clicked, and I'd welcomed her into the fold of my freelance buddies. I'd asked the universe for a sign, and the universe had answered. I would go, but I needed to be authentic. I had yet to publicly announce that I had gone in-house, and I couldn't go to ASJA pretending that I was still a full-time freelancer or that I didn't have a day job. So, I emailed Katherine to let her know I was going public with the job, I announced it on Facebook and LinkedIn the next day and garnered nothing but congratulations. I rolled around in them for a while before reminding myself that the only thing that mattered was whether I was, if not happy, not actively miserable.

I wasn't ready to walk away from the money and the psychic satisfaction that freelancing gave me, nor was I sure of how long my job at Digital Edge might last. If I stepped on Frank's toes again, not much longer. I took deep breaths and vowed to stay in my lane and to do my job. That was made easier by the fact that I was inundated with writing assignments. I was plowing through them when I received an email from Frank. I'd once again strayed from my lane. "It's the AM's responsibility to work with SEO if new keywords are needed, not yours," he wrote.

The week before, I'd been asked by Frank to participate in a client call with one of the AMs, and a client, a business that provided coaches who worked with seniors to help them maintain their cognitive function. The client wasn't happy with the content we'd produced, and when we got on the phone, the problem was clear. It wasn't an issue with the content per se but rather the keywords, which included phrases like "cognitive exercises for elderly."

I had already qualified for membership in AARP and written for Next Avenue, a website aimed at seniors, and knew a word like *elderly* was verboten. I wasn't surprised when the client pushed back on it.

"I understand your concerns, but those phrases are keywords," I said to the client. "Even though you don't use the word *elderly*, that's the word that people might use when searching for the kinds of services that you provide." We talked for a few minutes.

"With keywords like this, sometimes I say that 'you have to have to dance with who brung you,'" I said. "So, we can use those keywords because we have to but we can write content around them to downplay them." She insisted we avoid the word *elderly* completely. So after the call, I had walked over to Nick's desk, and we'd talked about swapping in different keywords. We'd talked it through, I'd emailed Taylor, and Nick had sent me new keywords (without the word *elderly*), which could then be used to rewrite the page. Problem solved, right? Not quite. Frank reminded me that any issues concerning keywords or strategy were the bailiwick of SEO and/or Taylor, the AM, but certainly not mine.

I wasn't used to being punished for being collaborative or helpful. Worse, I could see that the longer I was there, the more threatened he was becoming—and I had only been there less than three months. It was bound to get worse as time went on unless I could figure out how to simply do my job.

I did like working with Melissa and had told Molly, my therapist, that I was enjoying training her. "Well, don't teach her everything," Molly said.

I thought she was kidding.

"I'm serious," she said. "Don't teach her everything. Don't show her everything. You don't want her to be able to do your jo at less money than you get paid to do it."

"To be fair, I don't think I can show her everything," I said. "I do have 20 years of experience." Yet, how much was that experience really worth? I had suffered some blows to my ego recognizing that I was making a mere $45,000 at the age of now 53, with 20+ years of experience in my industry. When I thought that way, it was maddening. I had to keep coming back to, "but it's helping my anxiety" when I thought about how much more I could be making.

Frank had dumped three more rush assignments on me that morning, and I'd cheerily replied, "got it!" to each one. I missed the easy banter we'd had when I first started working there. I'd felt a connection with Frank, like we were simpatico, with a shared way of looking at the world. I liked smart people. I liked smart men. I'd thought we were peers. Equals. Friends even. Until I'd stepped wrong, and I'd realized that we weren't friends. He was my boss, and I was his subordinate. He was my boss. That was it.

He'd given Melissa a writing assignment—a fun, fluffy blog post on why you should carry a notebook. I had written books on freelancing, after all. It was a great fit for me, but I didn't get it. Then, he gave me another blog piece, due by week's end, on motivational quotes and study habits. I was excited at the idea of covering it—but I'd misread the email. It, too, was meant for Melissa.

Was I being punished? Perhaps. Around 2:00 p.m., he emailed and told me his legal writer had taken a full-time job and that he might have to use me for some legal writing assignments. "No problem!" I replied. "As long as I don't have to put on a suit and go to court, it's all good."

Stay in your lane, I reminded myself. Take it one day at a time. By Thursday, however, I was finding it hard to focus, let alone stay in the moment. I hadn't slept well the night before, hadn't made it to the gym, and was feeling fat and gross. My right hip had been bothering me. I hadn't been able to run in more than a week, and my anxiety was starting to climb.

Short List of Random Things That Make Me Anxious on Any Given Day

1. Facebook.
2. Not being on Facebook.
3. Getting older.
4. My mother getting older.
5. My children.
6. Thinking about my children driving.
7. The future of Social Security.
8. School shootings.
9. Workplace shootings.
10. Public shootings.
11. Gun nuts (see 8, 9 and 10).
12. Gravity. (Or more specifically, gravity's effect on my physical self.)
13. The stock markets.
14. My retirement.
15. Being unable to retire.
16. The idea of my adult kids living in my basement.
17. The idea of living in my adult kids' basement.
18. The state of the world.
19. Our current president.
20. The future.

At home, I'd been kicking around the idea of getting a dog, without sharing that with the kids. Erik and I had had dogs during most of our marriage. We'd brought home our first golden, Sandy, after I moved in with him. After she died, we got another golden, a maniac named Sugar Cookie. When we divorced, Erik got Sugar, and I took the cat, Pepper, whom we'd rescued a couple of years prior. I'd brought home a rescue puppy, Jordan, six months after getting divorced, agreeing to share her with Erik, but she'd been hit by a car while at his house. Neither of us had been ready to consider getting another dog.

I knew the kids wanted one, and I knew all of the benefits of having a dog. The issue was one of responsibility. I already felt overwhelmed sometimes. Could I handle the demands of a puppy and all that it entailed? Once again, I asked the universe for direction. What did I see that morning? A memory on Facebook from 10 years prior of Sandy as a puppy playing with a toy hamburger. That had to be it.

I'd talked it over with Walt, who had cautioned me about taking on more responsibility. "It's a big decision," he'd said. "You have a lot of plates spinning already."

Well, duh. Thanks, Captain Obvious. Any mom, especially a single one, spins plates all day long. That's what we do. It was one more way that we were different: I had a slew of responsibilities on any given day, and he only had himself to take care of. He didn't understand that my kids factored into nearly every decision I made and that the primary reason I was willing to take on the responsibility was for them and because of them.

That Wednesday was one of the days that draggggggged. I checked my computer screen, and it was only 9:27 a.m. when I'd been hoping it was nearly lunchtime. I methodically worked my way through six rewrites for a Canadian client that sold carpet and window "coverings" (not "treatments"), incorporating additional commodities and services, and making sure to use the word *colour* in place of *color*. After lunch, I stopped by Sarah's desk to say "hi." We'd spoken a few times, mostly about pieces of content she was editing, and I liked her.

When I got back to my desk, I emailed her a brief note, asking if she was up for a drink after work sometime. She sat just six feet diagonally behind me, but email felt safer. If she said "no," it wouldn't be to my face.

Her response was immediate and positive. "I'd love that!"When I responded with, "how about tonight," she was in.

A coworker date! Finally! We met at Cadence and sat at the end of the U-shaped bar, sipping wine. I jumped right in. "So, what do you think about Digital Edge?"

She took a sip of wine. "Is this conversation strictly between us?"

"Well, yeah! Like anyone else there even talks to anyone?"

Sarah cackled. "Oh, my God! No one talks! It's so quiet!"

"I know," I said. "The only sound you hear is the barely audible noise of keyboard tapping and that of my soul slowly dying." We both laughed. "I call it the morgue," I added. "Except that a morgue might have more action."

"I'm actually writing an essay about being an invisible woman," said Sarah. "I've never worked at a place where you can come and go, and no one even says hello or goodbye. These people are Automans! They just work in silence."

She was right. There was more interaction on the sales side, where I sat, for which I was grateful. The SEO guys engaged in some conversation, from what I could tell, but a good half of the office staff, if not more, sat at computers with headsets or headphones on, interacting with no one but their screens. "I thought the office would be more fun," she said.

"Like basketball hoops and people talking and joking around. There's none of that!"

"Yeah, I was expecting ping pong tables and pinball machines! I thought the same," I commiserated. "I expected an office of mostly Millennials to be hyper-connected. Yet, they all seem disconnected."

Sarah shook her head. I'd thought she was happy sitting quietly editing all day, but she'd been starving for stimulation, too.

"You're like a breath of fresh air," she said. "You're way more outgoing than I am. I'm surprised Frank hasn't said anything about you talking to everyone."

"Well, I have to interact with the SEO guys to do my job," I countered. But again, she was right. I looked for opportunities to talk, to connect. I wanted to be able to participate in the sales guys' banter. I wanted to talk. I wanted to laugh. I wanted to connect. There wasn't much of that at work.

The conversation eventually turned to money. While I knew discussing salaries was against company policy, I also already knew what she was making because Frank had offered me the editor job she now had. When I told her I made what she did, she was shocked. "I would think you'd be making at least $60,000!"

I was offended by my salary all over again, but I didn't want to admit that. "Yeah, but I didn't take this job just for the money," I countered. "The health insurance is huge, and I haven't had a 'real job' for 22 years, so I'm pretty sure I was unemployable."

Sarah nodded. She told me she'd been freelancing but looking, unsuccessfully, for a full-time job for several years before she started at Digital Edge. "My age is a factor," she said. "And then there's the whole issue of being hired by a 35-year-old. Being a woman doesn't help, either."

She said she'd taken the job because she was sliding into some bad habits and her husband wasn't working at the moment. I respected her space and backed off from the subject. We talked more about Frank and his territoriality. "Poor Frank," she said. "He hired both of us, and now's he discovered that we aren't 20-somethings who will just do what we're told."

We laughed, and I was surprised at how much I was enjoying talking to her. Finally, a like mind! We spent a couple of hours talking, laughing, and sharing stories about our writing lives thus far and agreed to do it again soon.

That Saturday, I drove to Peet's to start on Nancy's book, which had sold to a big publisher. I was caught up on other freelance work, but had the usual mélange of malaise that accompanied starting any major project—anxiety about getting it done, annoyance that I had to do it, and a tinge of excitement about the challenge, along with a new ingredient: random bitterness that I wasn't independently wealthy and could "just" work (and not have to freelance as well). I worked for about three hours before I hit a mental wall and realized I was done for the day.

Writing a book came down to filling up pages with words—at least 40,000 words, per our contract. That wasn't bad in terms of length, as typical trade books came in at about 70,000 to 80,000 words. I had written a robust proposal already, and by the end of the morning, I had about 5 percent of the book written. When I finished that chapter, I'd be more than 10 percent of the way there. There was still a lot of work to do, but I'd given my word, signed the contract, and couldn't back out, so I'd just have to "make it work," per fashion expert Tim Gunn. I could do that, too.

A lot had happened in the last three days. I'd decided to follow through on an idea that had been brewing for several weeks and had asked Frank if I could plan on working from home on Tuesdays and Thursdays. I said that I was confident that I could get my work done just as efficiently at home and that being at home two days a week would let me spend less on childcare. Might as well play the single mom card when I could.

Frank's response was brief: "Works for me."

All I had to do was ask! Maybe that was the sign I'd been waiting for. After all, now I'd be home four days a week (including the weekends) and at the office for three. I drove to the vet where they housed shelter animals and followed the receptionist into the kennel, where about a dozen dogs of all sizes barked as soon as we came in. A small black puppy sat dejectedly, her head down. She was wearing the "cone of shame," as was her little sister, the puppy next to her, who jumped up and wagged her tail when I approached. I asked to meet both of them, and the depressed puppy came to life in the little room, bouncing over and climbing into my lap. She wagged her tail and licked my face. Uh-oh!

I stopped by Erik's on the way home and told him I had decided to go ahead with the dog and confirmed that he was willing to help with her. We introduced the kids and Pepper to the puppy that evening. Pepper was less than pleased at meeting the puppy (not to mention the indignity of the kennel itself), and the puppy wasn't sure what to think of the cat. The kids were in. Erik was in. Once my paperwork was approved, I would once again be a dog owner.

I'd listened for the universe and trusted it when it whispered "yes." Or maybe it had whispered, "why not?" Whatever it was, I'd embraced the decision. By taking on a dog, a puppy at that, I'd effectively said that I believed things would be okay. That I would have enough money for a dog. Enough time. That I had enough available bandwidth to love another creature and that I could add to my daily quotient of shit-I-gotta-do. I realized that in trusting the universe and taking on one more thing, I was saying, "yes." "Yes" to whatever was next.

The Corporate Newbie's Cheat Sheet: How to Not Piss Off Your Boss in the First Two Months of Work

If you're like me, you believe that relationships matter. Even if you don't, keep this in mind: the relationship with your boss is the most important one you have at your job. Tend to it. Foster it. Do what you can to avoid making a mistake that will haunt you for weeks—or even months.

The best way to do this is to figure out your boss as best as you can. How much feedback does she expect from you? Does she want you to keep her apprised of what you're working on, or would she rather not be pestered by you? What's his communication style? Does he prefer to communicate primarily via email, through Zoom calls, or face-to-face meetings? What are his biggest priorities? How can help him achieve them? How can you make her look good?

Answering these questions will help you determine how you can make your boss happy—and help reduce the risk of making a rookie mistake that makes you look (and probably feel) shitty.

CHAPTER 6

Synergy

At work, I'd been assigned to a project for Sean, writing hub pages for a number of clients that needed them, and I had neglected to tell Frank that it had started. We'd discussed it several weeks prior, but I hadn't told him it was underway. The process was simple: the SEO analyst for the client would send me an email, giving me the URL and the pages that the hub page would link to, such as the different industries a company worked in or the types of clients it served. Then, I'd write 100-150 words of content about the company and include a bulleted list of the relevant pages that were used to build out the new hub page.

It wasn't complicated, but each page took some time as I had to familiarize myself with the client and come up with new content that wasn't duplicative of what was already on its site. Much of SEO writing was not writing but rewriting—using different words to say essentially the same thing on a different page. Google would ding you if you have the same content on more than one page, so as a writer I had to put on my thesaurus hat and get creative.

The issue with that was that sometimes I truly could not tell what clients did. A company might provide "strategic and technical offerings," "offer thought leadership and technical expertise," or "deliver impactful results" and yet I couldn't nail down exactly what the client did. Nearly every company claimed to be in the business of offering solutions of some kind but used rafts of business-speak to describe said solution. As a result, the pages took longer than expected, except for companies that sold products, rather than services, like the client that offered food safety classes to restaurant and food service workers, the client that specialized in custom socks for athletic teams, or the client that sold and installed fences throughout the Chicago area. Those were easier and gave me a brief reprieve from the murkier B2B solutions (again!) providers.

Frank and I had talked about the hub page project a week prior, but I had neglected to tell him I had started on it. I asked to meet with him offline, in Yahoo, and apologized for any unintended (which hopefully went without saying) breach in protocol.

"I should have notified you that the hub page project was beginning, and that's on me for not doing so. I'm keeping a list of the sites I'm doing," I said. "I'm sorry about that. Would you prefer that I send them to you as I do them, or is it easier if I just send the final list when I get done with it? That's what I was thinking would be more convenient, but however you want to do it is fine."

Yes, I was apologizing. Again! Apparently having this job meant apologizing. A lot. Sarah and I had discussed this. We were becoming friends, and even if it was because we were in the same asylum with a similar diagnosis, I was grateful. Like me, she'd gotten in trouble for mis-stepping with Frank, and we shared the nuggets of information we'd gleaned from our mere months of working there. I called them FMS, for Frank Management Strategies.

"He's very territorial," she said. "And man, do I say, 'I'm sorry!' a lot!"

"Same. I have said 'I'm sorry' more at this job than I ever have before," I agreed. It didn't matter that we are living in the #metoo era. Apparently, the two of us were caught up in an apologetic tailspin that seemed impossible to shake.

"I think you could have a career there," said Sarah.

"I'm not sure what that would look like," I said. "I don't want Frank's job, managing all that content. Or Roger's job! And I don't want to be an editor. No offense," I added.

"None taken! You get a lot more variety than I do."

"What's your end game?" I asked her. "At Digital Edge?"

"I don't know," she admitted. "Today, I wanted to quit."

I hadn't yet wanted to quit. I'd been pissed off before, and annoyed, and bored beyond belief, and I'd questioned plenty of my life choices, but I hadn't wanted to quit. I liked having a job. I liked not having to freelance anymore (except, oh, yeah, I was still freelancing and writing a book in my so-called spare time) to pay my bills.

Nancy's book was due in four months, which meant I needed to get some solid work done. On Thursday, I worked all day from home, fed and walked the puppy, and then immediately picked up my personal Mac to put in some time on chapter one.

The first chapter of any project was the most critical. For the prescriptive nonfiction I specialized in, it described the problem facing the reader, drew the reader in, and underscored the gravity and extent of said problem before eventually introducing the promise, the solution, of the book. I'd managed to expand the 1,500 words from the proposal into 5,600 words the Saturday before, but the chapter was still flabby and needed work. (Sort of like me.) I poked at it for about an hour, finishing a couple of sidebars before I left for an appointment with Scott, my chiropractor.

I'd been seeing Scott for several years. More than 30 years of running on a body that wasn't built for running meant that every few months something went awry. My right hip hurt. My right knee hurt. Or my back started bothering me. I'd sit on his examining table and describe what was bothering me, and he'd put his hands on me and adjust me, stretching, manipulating, and pressing down on bundles of nerve fibers until I moaned. The treatments were sometimes uncomfortable, but I always felt better afterwards.

I sat there, swinging my feet, running down the last week. "My hip was bothering me, so I didn't run for the last couple of weeks," I told him as he gently probed my left foot. "I had a good run on Monday, but my foot started hurting afterwards and has been swollen and sore since then."

"It sounds like a stress fracture," Scott told me. "It may not show up on an X-ray, but I'd like you to have one anyway."

I waited. "Does this mean no running?"

He patted my foot, rolling back in his chair. "Do you want to run right now?" he said, pointing at my foot, which was clearly swollen.

"Not right this second," I admitted and sighed. "How much time off are we talking about?"

"Probably about 12 weeks. You've got to give the bone a chance to heal."

Twelve weeks? I swallowed and tried not to cry. "I just got a puppy!" I said. "What about walking?"

"Stay off of it as much as you can," he said. "I'd say fewer than 5,000 steps per day. You should be staying off of it and icing and elevating it as much as possible. I'm going to wrap it and give you a walking boot to take some of the pressure off of it in the meantime." I nodded and agreed, but I was already spinning.

I'd managed my stress, and my weight, for years with my runs. A week or two off, I could handle. The idea of 12 weeks—almost 3 months—was alarming, but the next morning, I skipped the Y, following Scott's direction to stay off my foot as much as possible. Even so, it continued to swell throughout the day, and by that night at pool, I was limping badly. I lost a match I should have won, came home, iced it for a while, and crawled into bed, feeling sorry for myself. The one plus was that the dog and the kids were at Erik's. All I had to do for the next few days was take care of myself, work, finish chapter one for Nancy by Saturday, and get my foot X-rayed. That was manageable.

As for running? It was only for a few weeks, not forever. Yes, running was my tool of choice when it came to managing my stress. It was better than sex. Better than laughter. Better than wine, food, or even a great night's sleep. Running didn't just manage my stress; it produced a feeling of calm focus that nothing else could.

But Scott had okayed me biking once the swelling went down, and I could lift. I could use this time as an opportunity to strength-train more, rebuild my body, and slow down a bit. I could start doing yoga again. I could learn to meditate and stick with it this time! I could write about this miserable time and sell an article or essay about it.

My innate optimism forced me to reframe the situation even while my foot continued to hurt and I had to lurch around the office in a walking boot with Velcro that crackled whenever I moved. "Hurt doesn't mean harm," Scott had told me before, and I clung to that. I was injured, but my body would heal. I could manage this. I'd been through worse. I just needed to listen to my doctor, slow down, and take advantage of this opportunity … to learn something more about myself. Reframe, reframe, reframe.

As the days passed, however, I found it harder to maintain my positive attitude. My foot continued to hurt though I stayed off of it as much I could. I'd expected to see some improvement by this point, but so far there was none. My usual optimism had vanished, and I was caught up in a pity party of epic proportions.

Part of it was the pain, and part of it was the worry about the pain. I'd been injured before. I'd broken my ankle, had several rounds of plantar fasciitis, a bout of Achilles tendonitis, and issues with both my right hip and right knee for years. Shit, I'd fallen at Chuck E. Cheese and broken my wrist two years before!

But before I'd been able to do something physical, even if it was just pedaling slowly on the exercise bike or walking on the treadmill. Now, I was stuck lurching around the office, crackling with Velcro and despair, eating too much, drinking too much, and generally feeling sorry for myself. All of my high-brow intentions about rising to the challenge disappeared like smoke in the breeze.

I'd also conveniently repressed the fact that having a puppy means being awakened in the middle of the night, often more than once. After three nights in a row of getting up with Jetty, I was exhausted, irritable, and questioning my willingness to say yes to the universe. Maybe I needed to start saying no instead.

I reminded myself of that again, when Jet lunged at Haley, scaring her. "She thinks you're a puppy, honey," I told my daughter as the puppy nipped at her. I comforted her and gave Jet a toy she could chew on. "She's just trying to play with you."

The days I was home, I sat with my foot propped up on a pillow and iced it as often as I could. Eventually, the pain started to ease, and the swelling was also beginning to subside. Proof of healing, I told myself. Proof of progress.

I'd gotten used to the boot by now, and had my foot propped up on the barstool at Cadence when Sarah and I met for drinks. I'd spent the day head-down, banging out outlines. Melissa had produced almost twice as many outlines as I had in the past month. I'd had the hub page project for Sean and several dozen rewrites for Frank, but I still worried about my production compared to hers.

I was beginning to realize I couldn't do as much as I'd expected. Writing a book from scratch in my spare time was more than I could handle. Add in work, the kids, the puppy (I could now admit that had been a bad idea), and the fact that I was still hobbling and unable to run, and I was starting to feel like I was drowning.

Earlier that day, Frank had called a meeting with Roger, Melissa, and me to talk about outline production and any changes we could make to the process to make it smoother. He also announced that the company was hiring another copywriter. That meant our department would have to outsource less work to freelancers, saving money. It also meant that there would be less in the budget for any potential raise.

I pointed that out to Sarah, the only person I could discuss salary with, as we caught up over glasses of wine. "I was thinking about your salary," she told me. "I made that for Patch when I was an editor. Ten years ago."

"You made $45,000? Working for Patch?" Patch was a hyper-local website that presumably had a tiny budget.

She nodded and sipped her chardonnay. "Ten years ago."

"I have been living in the monkey house," I said. "Tim Gunn said it years ago on Project Runway." I explained. "When you first go into the monkey house, you're like, 'Wow, it stinks in here!' Then, you're there for a while, and you're like, 'Well, it smells but not that bad.' And then, you don't notice the smell at all because you're living in the monkey house."

I sighed and slugged back some of my wine. "That's it! I'm definitely asking for a raise at six months," I told Sarah. "I'm worth more than this, but if we're hiring another writer, doesn't that mean that there will be less in the department's budget for raises? You're splitting the same pie into more pieces."

Sarah agreed.

"They're probably going to give me a raise of like $2,000," I said. "And then what?"

She shrugged.

"I should be making $60,000," I said.

"That's what I thought, too," she said. "But you know they can find someone else to do my job and your job—someone just out of college—and pay them even less, but they won't have our experience."

"They may not even have some of the things you and I take for granted. Like showing up on time. Being professional," I said. "Having conversations with other humans," I added, snickering.

"This is the only place I've worked at that is so disconnected," Sarah said.

"You know, I'm going to outgrow this job," I said.

"Yeah! By the summer," said Sarah.

"Hell, by next Tuesday!" We cackled.

"No, by Friday, the next day after the day you work from home," she countered.

She was right. Still, there was much to like about my job. But I didn't just have a job. I had a book deadline, too. While I had 6,700 words down and the first chapter in the can, I was feeling resentful and overwhelmed. The foot (I'd started it calling it "the foot" as if it were no longer an actual part of my body) didn't help. It wasn't only that I couldn't run. It triggered fear every time I wiggled my toes and felt a twinge of pain. It's healing. It's healing. It's healing! I chanted to myself. To facilitate that healing, I had to do the opposite of everything I normally did—move less, do less, slow down, and ask for help instead of giving it.

My trip to New York would be a good time to reboot, pardon the pun. I did need to make the most of my time there. I had seven short pieces to write for one of my regular clients and wanted to make more headway on Nancy's book. That meant I'd have to work on the plane on the way there and possibly for a while when I first arrived. If I got enough accomplished—say, drafts of the articles and another 2,000 or 3,000 words of the next chapter of Nancy's book—I'd feel comfortable taking the rest of the time to talk, laugh, and catch up with my tribe. In the past, I'd used the conference to meet with editors and agents and to attend panels to keep up with changes in the freelance landscape. This year my focus was to connect, especially with my FOKs (Friends of Kelly).

My first priority? To spend quality time with my friend Jennifer, who was flying in from Florida and would be meeting two of her half-siblings for the first time earlier that day. Adopted as a baby, she'd stumbled onto her birth father's family after she had her DNA analyzed, discovering that she was a likely sibling of a woman who turned out to be her younger half-sister. She and I stayed up late that first night, talking, sharing, and crying, and then talking and laughing some more. I fell asleep, feeling grateful for my decision to come. To show up.

The next morning, Jen and I took the elevator down to the lower level of the conference, and I hugged and greeted a dozen or so people. The room hummed with energy, talk, and laughter. I'd come to this event nearly every year out of the last two decades, excited about the idea of meeting an editor who might become a new client, of learning something that I could use for my business, of jumpstarting my enthusiasm for freelancing when it flagged. Now I felt out of place. One of the opening keynoters talked about the need for better health insurance for freelancers, and I doodled in my notebook. I had no skin in this particular game now that I had gone in-house. I skimmed through the list of panels over the next few days, but without any real interest.

During a break, another writer I knew waved me over, surprising me with a hug. I didn't know Caitlin that well, but we'd been in ASJA together for years, spoken on panels together, and stayed in touch through Facebook. She was a much bigger name than I, writing for *The New York Times,* among other high-profile markets.

"I'm so glad you're here!" she said. "I wanted to thank you again for that bracelet." I'd forgotten that last year I'd sent her one of my intention bracelets when she was being treated for breast cancer. Her word had been *onward.* She pulled out her phone and showed me a picture of a stuffed rhino with the bracelet around its neck.

"That's how I handle things," she said, pointing at the rhino. "I run right at them." I laughed and handed her back the phone.

"I wore it all the time," she continued. "I couldn't wear it during surgery, but I had it with me," she said. "It's so nice to have an actual thing."

"It's a talisman," I agreed. "I'm so glad it helped, even a little." I asked about her recent book proposal, which she'd mentioned on Facebook, and she said an editor was looking at it.

"Didn't you write *Malled*?" I asked, recalling her memoir about working in the retail industry.

"I did!" Our talk turned to other subjects, and I wished her the best with her book. I walked back to my table, reminded that one small act could make a difference to someone. I sat down next to Jennifer and realized I no longer felt out of place. I wanted to be here. More important, I wanted to be here next year—to pitch the book idea I'd been kicking around, which I'd privately titled, *The Book that Got Me Fired*.

I'd arrived confident that this was likely my last ASJA conference. Now I had ping-ponged back to wanting to continue keeping my freelance career alive. I attended several panels throughout the next two days, including a pitch slam on how to write for markets for people 50+. I pitched my idea—on what to do and not do when you started a new job in your 50s. It was too late for me to make a new first impression at work. Like it or not, the office knew me (or was beginning to know me) as talkative, loud, and usually friendly.

Still, I could write about what to do for other people. How meta! Later that day, I moderated a panel on ghostwriting, which featured my agent, Katherine, and three book editors. All four women were smart and insightful, offering plenty of advice and examples to the attendees. Afterward, Katherine and I had drinks with two of them, and they sat there chatting about recent deals, books that had gone to auction and authors they were working with. I felt that familiar tug. These were my people! Not the Automans at work. I wasn't young enough, cool enough, well-informed enough, or even well-read enough to hang with them—but I wanted to. Populating spreadsheets and creating SEO-driven content wasn't anywhere near as sexy and engaging as ghostwriting books for a living. I'd thought I was done freelancing? Wrong!

I talked to Bill about it the next morning. A charming, smart, multifaceted man I'd known and respected for years, Bill, at 64 was happily retired. We talked for a few minutes about where we were at in our lives.

"I thought I didn't want to freelance anymore, but I still want to have something to aspire to," I said. "My job doesn't give me that."

"I've given up on aspirations," he said with a laugh. "My goal now is to do things I want to do for the doing. I wrote books for 20 years, but I've never written a book I'd want to read!"

"Can you afford that? Can you afford to be retired?"

'It's a frugal retirement, but yes."

I shook my head. "I've got a long way to go before retirement," I said.

"Well, yes, until your kids are out of college," he said.

I hadn't done the math until that moment. Haley was only nine and in third grade. She had nine years of school left, plus four years of college if she made it there. That meant I had 13 years—at least 13 years!—left to work. What was I going to do with those 13 years? How was I going to make the most of my 13 years (or more)?

My conversation with Bill the day before was still playing through my mind during the flight home. Thirteen years. Thirteen more years of work. It was such a long time. Yet, Ryan had been a gummy, drooling, cuddly toddler seemingly yesterday, and now he was a cocky, confident high school freshman. I had to work, but I wanted more than that. How could I take advantage of this time and pay my bills while I also saved for retirement and for college? How could I enjoy the day-to-day more while making room for more adventures and experiences with the kids? What did I want for myself?

What did I want for our family? On the plane, I made a list of what I wanted in the months to come:

Reasonable, Achievable, Doable Goals for Spring and Summer

1. Heal my foot. That was presumptive as I couldn't do the healing. I amended it. Let my foot heal.
2. Get back into a good workout and eating groove. I'd been overeating, over-drinking, and under-exercising. I didn't feel good in my body right now, and I wanted to reset that.
3. Be more present with the kids. I'd been crabby, disconnected, and overwhelmed of late. They expected so little from me, and yet sometimes I wasn't even delivering that.
4. Have more adventures with the kids. Ryan was already pulling away from me, which was normal and expected but also a little heart-breaking. I didn't have that much time to create memories with them before they grew up. I'd heard so many people raving about *Hamilton*, I'd decided to take the kids and Walt, as a special treat.
5. More connecting with friends and people who mattered to me. I'd been holed up for the last few weeks, overwhelmed with the responsibilities I felt, when connecting with people was how I rebooted.
6. A greater sense of calm. Not waking up feeling exhausted, overwhelmed, and cranky. A sense of balance. I liked being excited. I liked energy. I was attracted to it, even bad energy. But calm seemed like a more manageable goal.

When I returned from New York, I had that familiar sense of returning to the ordinary. The week passed. The kids came home from Erik's, I worked, parented, took care of the animals, and stayed off the foot as much as possible. The first morning back at work, I received an email from one of the AMs, asking about a blog I was writing for a client that rented industrial equipment. She wanted to know if it was possible to have it completed by week's end. I emailed her back without stopping to think about it, cc-ing Frank, who was working from home. I told her my deadline but that she'd have to ask Frank about when the piece would be through editing.

One minute later, Frank sent me a one-line email that said, "Let's meet about this on Friday."

Dammit! I'd done it again. Or had I? I hadn't told Genevieve when she could expect it back from editing; just that I was turning the piece in that day, so she'd at least know that it was in the works. I tapped out a quick reply, apologizing for revealing my deadline, but pointing out that I had left the delivery date up to him. He didn't reply to that email, but sent a group email to the entire team, reminding us that we were to refer any questions about assignments, scheduling, or delivery to him—and that we were not to provide updates or promise any deadlines.

The email was obviously meant for me, and a familiar surge of anxiety hit. This wasn't supposed to happen at work! Work was supposed to help me manage my anxiety, to keep it under control. I reread the emails. I had revealed information about a content deadline, which meant I had once again screwed up.

I didn't want another talking-to, and I also didn't want to apologize again. I'd done that in my email already. I went out into the hall and called Walt, who had been laid off from work that day and was home.

"This is bullshit," I whispered angrily, pacing up and down the hallway. "I want to quit." I was 53, and I was "in trouble" at work for failing to obey a rule that, let's face it, I thought was stupid. It was about territory and power—namely, Frank's. I thought it was a stupid rule, so I'd ignored it. Not consciously— I'd responded to the email too quickly for that—but I had ignored at least the spirit of the rule, which was that Frank was the boss.

I'd thought I had outgrown the job a month ago. I knew Melissa could do my job. The things that I was good at—relationship-building, brainstorming, connecting—weren't valued here. That's why I'd told the AM I'd have the blog done—so that she could relax. Now I had 48 hours to twist myself into a miserable pretzel, waiting for my talking-to.

The next morning, at Peet's, I filled in the guys at my table on the latest. I'd started calling them my executive board. "So, my boss is meeting with me tomorrow morning as a result. Any advice?"

Sy started to say something, and I shook my head. "I don't need any sarcastic or smartass comments that are less than helpful right now" I said pointedly.

But Sy, usually the quickest with a pointed and sometimes amusing piece of repartee, surprised me. "Ask yourself what outcome you want to have from this meeting," he said. "And ask your boss that—what outcome does he want from the meeting."

I nodded. "That ... that's actually really good advice."

Sy continued. "He's going to tell you to keep your mouth shut and do your job."

"Pretty much," I agreed. "But this isn't about what I did wrong. I value relationships. I'm trying to create relationships with the people I work with," I said. "My immediate reaction was to simply answer her and help her out. It was only after I sent the email that I knew I'd screwed up. Again," I added.

Later, it occurred to me that if I valued relationships, I needed to work on mine with Frank. He was my boss, after all. My relationship with him was arguably the most important one I would have at work—at least at this position—and I wasn't helping myself by straying outside of his prescribed lanes.

It also wouldn't help me to be snarky or disrespectful the next morning when I got my dressing-down. Another executive member I thought of as Bill the boat builder (not Bill the benefits guy or Bill the insurance guy—there were a lot of Bills at Peet's) offered me some advice. "May I tell you something?"

"Of course," I answered.

"I don't think you're going to be at the company for very long," he said. "You've been self-employed for too long."

"But ... health insurance!" I said. Always my go-to answer. Later that morning, I talked to Jordan about it and admitted that I was afraid I would cry tomorrow. I hadn't said that to the men. "It's the sheer injustice of it all," I explained. "That frustration. That's what sets me off. I start to react, and the next thing I know, I'm in tears. I hate it."

She nodded, tucking her long hair behind her ear. "Oh, I would do the same thing," she said. Mary, who was sitting at the end of the table paging through a travel magazine, chimed in. "Me, too. Absolutely."

I went to work the next morning prepared for battle. I'd had my hair cut and blown out, and I was wearing one of my favorite dresses, the ever-present boot, and a black low-heeled platform sandal. I blasted "Muse" on the way to the office, mentally gearing up to bend but not break. Be a willow tree, I thought. Blow in the breeze. Sway. Bend. Flow. But I was still anxious, so I went into the nook, cut a Clonopin in half, and swallowed it with my coffee. It would numb my senses enough that I didn't think I'd cry. Then I waited … and waited … and waited.

Frank never asked to meet with me. I even made a point of turning in my chair to ask a question about meta descriptions to get a read on his mood, but he didn't bring it up. I worked, slowly but steadily. I took my usual lunch break, walking around the neighborhood adjacent to the office park, and returned to work, wondering if he was going to wait until the end of his workday, but he never called the meeting. I left for home feeling a little deflated. I'd been ready for the confrontation. I'd been prepared to be conciliatory, reasonable and yes, bendable without breaking down or apologizing profusely again. And the occasion hadn't arisen.

I told my therapist Molly about it at my next session, bringing her up to speed on my trip to New York. "I survived, even with the stupid boot on," I said. "And I had a blast." I told her about talking and laughing with Jennifer, about reconnecting with my freelance friends, about realizing that I had another book I wanted to write—The Book. I had gotten though a challenging stretch. Maybe not with any grace, but I had done it. That's what mattered.

"Did you have time to think about what you want? For yourself?" Molly reminded me.

My pat answer was that of every parent—for my kids to grow up to be happy (or, at least, somewhat content), productive, functioning humans. I was still nailing down what I wanted for myself.

"I want … I want my life to look like a forest," I said slowly. "Where there are a lot of trees but also undergrowth, and it's like a mesh," I explained. "Not a forest where it's just some trees standing there." Messy metaphors aside, I wanted substance. Connection, depth, a network of people, and interests, and stimulation, and experiences. Laughter. Intelligent conversations. Challenges. Things to look forward to, whether it was playing pool on Wednesday nights with my team, the annual trip to New York, the anticipation of warm summer days lying poolside with a book, simply meeting Sarah or Hannelore for a drink. I loved working hard and then taking time off and savoring it. I was learning to do that better at work.

"Yes. And not just one tree," Molly added. I knew she meant Walt. We'd talked before about my tendency to focus too much on the man in my life and let other aspects of my life dangle. I'd done that with my marriage for years, at least until Ryan was born and the entire framework of my life shifted and he, and later Haley, became the priority. I still wasn't sure whether Walt and I had a Future, and Molly's homework for me had been two-pronged: to identify what I wanted in a partner, and more important, get clearer about what I wanted for myself.

I told Hannelore about it on the way to Ronnie's mom's funeral on Saturday. Rhonda was one of our friends from college, and while she'd moved out to DC, she was coming home for the funeral. Hannelore and I drove into the city together. "So, as you can imagine, I have lots to write," I said, explaining that Molly wanted me to write down what I wanted in a partner.

"She asked that of a writer?" said Hannelore. "You're going to come in with a whole portfolio."

"Yes, with tabs organizing all of the information and dozens of Post-its," I said. "I can easily do 5,000 words on what I want and another 5,000 words on what my partner should have." I wanted someone who was warm, funny, and comfortable in his own skin. Someone honest, who cared about other people, and who wanted to help make the world a better place. Someone who was minimally emotionally damaged. Someone who took care of his physical health without being obsessed with it, someone without any serious addictive behavior (I saw far too many smokers and heavy drinkers at the pool hall), someone who liked his job but wasn't married to it. Someone with the ability to "conversate," my made-up word that meant the ability to talk about anything from human behavior to standup comedians to business strategy to home repair to shared experiences, the kind of conversation where you get to use your big, sexy words like plethora, indignities, and juxtaposition. Someone I was attracted to—and, obviously, who was good in bed. And had a nice smile. And made me laugh.

"I mean, really, that's it," I said to Hannelore after I realized my list had grown longer than expected and was straying into magical unicorn territory.

"Well, yeah. But what if you meet a guy who has all that but can't kiss?"

"Then, I'm out!" I said, laughing. Besides, kissing is the gateway drug to sex. If a man can't kiss, we're not going to go any further. If a man can kiss, though, lights turn green.

At the funeral, I hugged Ronnie, told her I was sorry, and introduced myself to her dad. We talked for a few minutes before the service. "I'm trying and trying, but I can't get her obituary written," said Ronnie.

"I'd be happy to write it for you," I said.

"Really?"

"Sure. I'll call you, talk to you and your dad, and write it up for you," I said. "It's no big deal. I've done them for a couple of other people."

"You can? You will?" Ronnie's face was expectant.

"That's why it helps to know a writer," said Hannelore.

Sitting there during the service, my mind wandered. I thought about my forest analogy and what I was missing in my life. I wanted more. Yet, I also wanted less.

"Forget what I want in a partner. You know what I really want?" I said to Hannelore on the drive back home. "To be free of anxiety. My biggest fear isn't being alone or not having a partner. It's that my mind will always be like this, spinning, whirling, and never shutting off, forever trapped with my own anxiety."

"Oh, I get it," said Hannelore. "It's like water eroding away granite. Oh, you've got to come up with $3,000 extra a month to take care of your mother-in-law, who's in assisted living, your mom had kidney surgery and then breast cancer, your brother almost lost his wife and baby, now you have chest pains and…" She waved her arms. "It's too much."

"See, I never think of you as an anxious person," I said. Hannelore was the epitome of a type B, one of the reasons we'd stayed friends.

"That's the thing! I don't feel anxious! You know my personality," she said. "But, apparently, I am."

It comforted me that Hannelore, one of the chill-est, most laid-back people I knew, confessed to anxiety as well. Maybe more people than I realized were dealing with the same thing—but quietly, to themselves, struggling and succeeding and failing the same way I was. Maybe we all were.

The Corporate Newbie's Cheat Sheet: How to Survive, and Even Make the Most of, an Important Meeting

Billions of hours (well, that's my estimate, anyway) and even more billions of dollars are wasted in work meetings every year. Regardless, though, you'll most likely spend at least part of your time in some. I'm a fan of taking notes, which makes you more likely to remember the most important takeaways from the meeting and (bonus) hopefully makes you look attentive and like you care what's happening. Unless you have something critical to share, I'm a fan of lying low for at least the first few meetings you have at your new job. Chances are no one is expecting that much from you at this point, anyway.

However, if it's a meeting of some import—like you're asking for a raise, your responsibilities are being changed, or you're reporting on your big project, you can't afford to stay mute. Use these steps to prepare for a critical conversation:

1. Know what your goal is. Do you need more help to get your work done? Are you going to ask to work from home more often? To change your hours? For a raise? For more responsibility? Or are you in trouble for making a mistake (oops), and your goal is to keep your job? Be very clear about what you want to achieve from the meeting.

2. Think about how your boss is likely to respond. By this point, you should have a bit of a read on your boss. If this is a proactive meeting where you're making a request, use what you know to anticipate how he or she is likely to respond, what obstacles he or she may raise, and what questions he or she may ask. If your boss has called the meeting, glean as much intel as you can about its purpose as you can beforehand. The more prepared you are, the more confident you will feel.

3. Practice your pitch. I'm a fan of one-way conversations with myself, but you aren't going to do this at work. Do it in your bathroom, on the way to work, or while walking your dog. Practice what you'll say and how you'll say it. Tinker with your language until you're asking for what you want without having to think about it. If you are facing a meeting where you fear

you'll have to defend yourself, then practice accepting responsibility for your screw-up (if it is yours) without getting tearful or angry. You can't control the emotions you may experience, but some practice can help prevent those emotions from overwhelming you.

4. Follow up after the meeting. You got what you wanted? Great! Send your boss an email saying thank-you and confirming what happened. You didn't get what you wanted? Send an email anyway, confirming what happened, so that you have an electronic paper trail if you need it. If the meeting was about a mistake and you owned it, it won't hurt you to send an email acknowledging your mistake, thanking your boss for his or her time, and promising to do better. (Because we know you will, right?)

CHAPTER 7

Retargeting

Now that summer was here, I was working from home three days a week. I'd asked for permission to do so in May, and Frank had okayed it. Working from home made it easier to run Haley back and forth to swim practice or sports camp or play dates; Erik covered me the days I was in the office. Ryan was old enough to ride his bike wherever he wanted to go and spent the morning at the pool and the afternoon playing X-box or at the park hooping with his buddies.

I still worried about being able to be as productive from home as I was at the office. At the office, I used a huge monitor that made our enormous spreadsheet easy to read and navigate and could save it on the company server in less than a second. At home, my laptop screen was less than half as big, and using the virtual private network that I used to work from home meant there was a lag when I hit "save" on my current work. The lag was only a few seconds, but I still worried that something might be lost during the pause between entering data into the spreadsheet and it being saved on the company network.

There was another issue I hadn't mentioned to Frank. If I had a question about one of the keywords or the relevant page, I walked over and pestered the relevant SEO analyst. If he didn't know the answer, which was rare, one of the other guys might lean back in his chair to chime in. They'd talk it through, and I knew I'd walk away with the answer I needed. At home, I'd send an email instead, but I missed the camaraderie I was starting to build with SEO; often, I learned more from listening to them talk back and forth than I could have gleaned from a sentence-long email response.

I liked that aspect of the job. I liked sitting and listening to the sales guys bullshit each other. I liked working side-by-side with Melissa. I even liked Frank and the rest of the content team enough, but much of the time I felt disconnected there. The more I worked from home (or from Peet's or from both), the more pronounced that disconnect became.

I craved community, and as I pulled away from my freelance friends, work wasn't filling the created gap. The SEO guys talked, joked, and laughed from the other side of the office. The sales guys, same things. There was some banter among the design team, but within the other departments—content, CMS, PPC—there seemed to be little interaction.

I was starting to suspect that there wasn't a position I could grow into at Digital Edge. Then, there was the question of money, or rather, the lack of money. I could just barely pay my bills thanks to what I received from Erik for maintenance and child support, but when I catapulted myself into the future, I could hardly breathe, imagining a world where my expenses had gone up and my salary had not (or not enough, anyway.) It felt like college was breathing on the back of my neck, but in the meantime, there were basketball shoes, sweatpants, and clothes for Haley, allowances, birthday party gifts, and things like buying *Hamilton* tickets for $700 for me, the kids, and my mom.

Because I was spending $700 to see *Hamilton*. I had resisted seeing the play for several years, even while seemingly all of my well-traveled, well-read, cultured writer friends in the New York area saw it. Then, it came to Chicago, and seemingly every family in the neighborhood, hell, the entire village of Downers Grove, went to see it. And still I didn't go. But my trip to New York had reminded me that experiences mattered. I thrived on the disruption of the everyday, of the ordinary. I loved making memories. I wanted to model that for the kids. So, what was I waiting for? Life was short, after all.

I often said to Walt, "If I dropped dead tomorrow, I'd want to make sure I'd [---] the day before," and I'd fill in the blank with whatever activity I was justifying or talking him into. Getting laid. Eating ice cream. Treating myself to a delicious meal.

"You know, that's kind of negative, the way you talk about dropping dead all the time," he'd pointed out.

"It's not negative! It's positive! It's life-affirming! It says that I'm choosing to do something instead of waiting or putting it off!" I was used to working hard and then rewarding myself with the proverbial carrot, whether that was with a glass of wine, a handful of M&Ms, an hour spent with a good book, or a romp with Walt. Or spending $700 to see *Hamilton*. I'd offered to buy Walt's ticket, but he had refused to go.

"I'm not really into 'musicals,'" he said, waving his hands around.

"What does that mean? And why are you making Bob Fosse hand gestures?"

He shook his head. "You know what I mean."

"It's not a musical. Well, it is, but it's not just a musical. It's Hamilton! It's supposed to be amazing. Haley's been listening to the soundtrack already," I said. "Even Ryan wants to go."

Although he had begged off, that hadn't stopped me. Instead, I invited my mom, who was thrilled. I bought the tickets and circled the date on my calendar, excited about having something to look forward to.

Atlanta had started to migrate the enterprise clients—the clients with the biggest budgets—over to Melissa and me. We'd then be responsible for outlines for all of the company's clients. I was ready for the challenge and had made solid headway on Nancy's book in the last few weeks, working nights and weekends to do so.

One thing nagged at me. I wanted to address the tension between Frank and me which seemed to have lingered since our conversation of a few months ago when I'd been instructed to stay in my lane. I'd talked to Gabriel about it a few days prior. "The vibe between us was weird," I said. "When he asked me if he'd ever said anything to indicate that he didn't value me? What is that? It sounded like we're in a relationship."

"You are in a relationship," Gabriel had countered. "Not a romantic relationship, but a relationship all the same. So, think about how you can manage that relationship."

How would I manage it? The way I'd manage any relationship—by being transparent and open. I thought about what I would say to Frank and how, and I'd thought about what I would say and how before the meeting that did not occur. Thanks to my executive board, I'd been prepared for a meeting where I had expected to have to defend myself. This was different. I was being proactive, deliberate.

I requested a meeting with Frank in Yahoo, I started the meeting by updating him on the progress Melissa and I had made on outlines, and expressing my confidence that we could handle the additional workload. Then, I launched into the meat of what I needed to address.

"I wanted to tell you that I really appreciate being able to work from home three days a week," I said. "It's made my summer much easier, especially with the kids. So, thank you."

Frank nodded, his arms folded across his chest.

"I also wanted to say that I am realizing that I may be … challenging to manage," I continued. "I haven't worked for a boss for a long time, and I'm still trying to figure out how to do that. Then, there's the whole issue of having someone 30 years younger than me who's doing my job and doing it well. It's unsettling. I'm trying to figure out how I can add more value here. Not only to you but also to the company as a whole. That's why I'm always asking questions, and why sometimes I have a hard time staying in my lane." I chose that phrase intentionally, hoping he would recognize that I was referring to our meeting in Google.

"But I am learning, and I am listening," I told him. "I realize we sometimes have different approaches to solving the same problem, and I respect that. I don't know that I want your job, but I like working for you. I like this company, and I think I may want to grow into a position of more authority and responsibility." I took a breath. "And I need your help to do that. I'd appreciate it if you'd let me know if there are things I can do—or not do—to help make that happen."

Frank's posture relaxed a bit. "You have to recognize that most of the employees have been more passive," Frank said. "They haven't wanted to know how all the different pieces work together or what the different departments do. I'm starting to understand how you work and how to turn that into a positive instead of a negative."

"I am trying to follow the rules," I said, without adding that I thought they were often stupid. "I also recognize that you have years of experience here and I only have a few months," I added. I didn't want to lay it on too thick, but I did need his help. No one else at the company, except Melissa, knew what I did all day or how valuable it was. If good kissing was the gateway to sex, Frank was the gateway to a raise and a future at the company. I needed to respect him, and, more important, make sure that he saw that I did so.

"It's no secret to you that I do want to make more money," I continued. "I will be asking for a raise. I need to make enough so I no longer need maintenance from Erik." Typically, I'd blurted out something inappropriate, personal, and none of his business. It was also true. Whether Walt and I stayed together, whether I was with any man, I didn't want Erik's money. Right now, though, I needed it. My goal was to make enough not to need maintenance and not to have to freelance anymore. Unless I wanted to. If I got a big enough raise, I should be able to do so.

I left the meeting with Frank feeling pleased with myself. I couldn't control how he reacted to me or to anyone, but I could be more thoughtful and more deliberate about how I managed our relationship. I was still doing a mix of writing and outlines, and I liked the variety. Occasionally, other projects were funneled to me, including coming up with blog ideas for clients for the CMS, or content marketing services, department if the content marketing specialist was having trouble doing so. I'd done plenty of this kind of brainstorming as a freelancer, and it was a nice break from my usual work. I'd read up on the client itself, do background research on possible topics, and then create a list with Google-unique blog titles and several resources for each one to make the writing process relatively simple. My goal was to create titles that were not only unique but also intriguing. I was aware that while we were always trying to please Google to achieve better SEO results (hence the unique title), it was in fact human beings who would eventually click through and (hopefully) read the content we created.

One morning, I spent several hours writing up the 7-step process I used to come up with blog ideas, using the most recent client as an example. It was intended to be a guideline for the content specialists, who sometimes had trouble creating blog post ideas for subjects they often knew little about. I had known nothing about automated warehouse equipment, including the fact that it existed, until I was given the assignment, but I knew how to research. That was a skill that could be learned. I emailed my process to Frank, who thanked me, and sent it to Sean. It would be up to the latter to share it with the CMS team if he saw fit.

Score! I'd provided Sean with one solid piece of evidence to back up my forthcoming request for additional pay—and I needed it. As of July 1, Erik's maintenance payments would drop by $600 a month. While child support would increase slightly, I was starting to worry, again, about money. I was glad I'd already bought tickets to *Hamilton*; now that I knew how much less I'd get from Erik, I would have never ponied up for them.

The day of the show, all four of us dressed up—even Ryan, who wore his suit jacket, tie, and dress pants, looking polished and handsome. Haley wore her favorite dress and asked me to straighten her hair so it hung sleek and shining over her shoulders.

The show was stunning: the music, the choreography, the hyper-fast rapping dialogue that blended history and humor, the music that swelled, the energy of the performers, the grace of their bodies, and the beauty of their voices blending together. Both kids were rapt. As was my mom. As was I. I'd been annoyed during the drive in heavy traffic and the wait to enter the crowded theater, then stressed by the time it took us to leave (in the back of my mind, I thought, what if there's a fire?), but it was worth it. Every penny!

That's what money was for—not only to pay bills but also to fund experiences. It bothered me that Walt had said no, but that hadn't stopped me. I'd said yes, and I was grateful again that yes was still my default.

At work, my responsibilities were continuing to grow. The day before, Frank had called me into a meeting in Yahoo despite the fact we'd met the week before. "We finally have the staff in place to do something Roger and I have wanted to do for a long time," he said. "We are in the position to have someone from the content team be on every kickoff call."

I waited. I was learning (slowly) to wait. "How would you feel about being that person? Are you amenable to that?" he continued.

"I'd love that," I said, calmly. "I think that would be a great use of my skills for the company." That's all I needed to say. But I couldn't help myself. Maybe I wasn't learning much after all. "This is great! This is what I suggested a couple of months ago," I added.

Frank chose to ignore that, and we discussed the mechanics of how the calls would work. Sean would invite me to kick-off calls via Outlook calendar, yet another technology tool I was mastering at DE. At some point during the call, I'd have an opportunity to introduce myself, talk to the client briefly about its current and future content, and then would share my notes with Frank. That info could then be added to the CGI (client general information) document, a huge Word doc that included background on all of our clients, including terms to use or avoid, grammatical preferences like whether they used the Oxford comma, and industry-specific language that writers should be aware of. The content team was expected to refer to the document before writing or editing for a client, though I didn't always remember to do so.

The kickoff calls were a step in the direction I wanted to move in. I liked the idea of doing more client-facing work as opposed to populating spreadsheets and churning copy for the rest of my days. Working as a ghostwriter for more than a decade meant I'd spent a lot of time on the phone with clients, talking about their book projects and equally important, listening. I listened not only to what they said but also to how they said it. That ability—to be able to capture someone's voice—was critical to ghostwriting and a skill I relied on to when I had to talk to DE clients who were displeased with the content we'd written.

I'd talk to them about what they weren't happy with and afterward fill in Frank, who then updated the GCI. Often, I wound up revising the content, using the feedback from the call to do so. If I were on the kickoff calls, I'd be able to glean firsthand what clients wanted, which increased the likelihood of delivering content that matched the client's expectations from the outset.

I was excited about the idea. It sounded like it would give me more responsibility as well as more variety. I wanted to be appreciated, to be valued, to have people respect me, and to respect what I could do. That's something I was missing in my job. There was a certain cachet to ghostwriting. People were impressed, interested, and even intrigued by what I did. The fact that I'd survived as a freelancer for 20+ years had earned me respect from random people (even if they had no idea what my job actually looked like), but plugging information into spreadsheets, writing 500-word blog posts, and revising content to make clients happy didn't impress anyone. I wasn't feeling particularly valued, especially when it came to my salary.

As I approached the six-month mark, I kept thinking, "talk is cheap." I was churning out outlines. I was churning out content. I was revising landing pages for clients who were hard to please, and now I might be stepping into a role that involved more client contact and therefore, presumably at least, more value to the company. That meant more money.

I was starting to think about myself as an employee now, a corporate drone, a working stiff. I didn't mind being a working stiff until I started comparing my salary to what I realistically should be making based on my experience—somewhere in the neighborhood of at least $60,000.

There was a question of ego here, too. I was embarrassed to admit that I was making "only" $45,000. I'd had some lean years as a freelancer, but that was different. I knew I was able to make six figures, or high five figures, because I'd done it. The years I'd made less money was because I'd had different priorities, like spending more time with my kids when they were little (I'd done that), to focus on other priorities like writing fiction (I'd done that), to start my own publishing business (done that), or to branch out in another field entirely—personal training (and I'd done that, too).

With a job, I was expected to, and was paid to, work 40 hours a week. I didn't have the freedom to work fewer hours to explore other options. That was the nature of a full-time job. I accepted that and needed to be paid more for the time I devoted to work. To do that, I'd have to prove my value. I hadn't had a problem doing this as a freelancer. I often asked for more money for assignments, justifying it with the fact that the story required a lot of background research, that it was a tight deadline, or that I'd been writing for the client for a while. Clients didn't always say yes, but often they did.

I needed to take a similar approach with my raise. The facts:

1. I had been hired to do one specific job (create outlines for clients, with a little bit of writing thrown in) and had been underpaid even for that specific job.

2. My job responsibilities had grown since I'd started. I was now writing a significant amount of content, producing reworks at the rate of 5-10 a month, and rewriting content that clients weren't happy with.

3. I'd created a couple of time-saving strategies that saved our department money as well, not to mention the template I'd created to help the CMS team develop ideas. That document alone was worth something.

4. I was being offered, and was taking on, more responsibility: participating in client calls, writing them up for the content team, and stepping in on calls where clients were not happy to address their content issues and hopefully redress them.

I made a list of what I'd accomplished in the last six months. I did some salary research. The figures I came up with, based on the type of work I was doing and my experience, ranged between $56,000 and $81,000 or more—proof that I was underpaid. The market might not matter to the purse string holders at the company, but I thought that the fact that I'd taken on so many additional responsibilities, including writing original content and reworking content pages that resulted in direct savings to the company (of arguably at least $12,000 to $15,000, possibly more) more than justified my raise.

It took me several hours to write my formal request. I believed in metrics, even if I hadn't been given specific metrics to aim for, so I noted plenty of numbers. I'd created 706 outlines for more than 150 clients. I'd optimized 111 pages on my own; between Melissa and me, we'd optimized 237 pages total, which represented a savings of at least $6,660 to the department as these pages hadn't needed to be assigned to freelancers. I'd also written 96 pages of original content, which I valued at $5,760.

I also noted that I'd revised 62 pieces of content, written the case study for the CMS department explaining how to come up with potential blog ideas, and that I was now participating in client calls. I'd written 27 hub pages for the SEO team and six e-com project briefs. I summarized the request with the fact that I believed that the scope of my job, the value of the work I'd performed, and my ongoing expansion of responsibilities merited a salary that was more in the range of $56,000 to 81,000. I closed my request with business-speak, thanking Frank for his time and consideration, and hit send.

Reviewing what I'd accomplished over the past months had confirmed that while I liked my job, I wasn't being paid enough for what I was doing. I wasn't sure that the partners understood what I did and its value, and I wanted them to recognize that the person who Frank had hired was smart, capable, and ambitious—and someone who deserved to be rewarded.

I thought I'd made it easy for them to say yes. The question was whether they would.

In the meantime, Scott had finally okayed me to start running again, more than two months after he diagnosed my latest running injury. "Remember, it probably took a long time to get to the point where you actually got a stress fracture," cautioned Scott as he gently prodded my foot. "Even though it's healed, if you looked at a bone scan, you'd see that that area is still very metabolically active. That means that your body is still rebuilding that bone.

"You can walk and then run for 30 seconds," he said. "Then, walk for a minute and run for 30 seconds again. The idea is to increase the stress on the bone very gradually."

The first time I gave my foot a try, I walked on the treadmill for a couple of minutes to warm up, then ran for 30 seconds, and walked again. The first few seconds of the run felt strange. I hadn't even walked fast for months. By the third interval, though, I had my legs under me. I did 20 minutes of brief running intervals and then walked briskly for another 20 minutes, jamming out to the *Hamilton* soundtrack.

The next morning, I stepped out of bed cautiously. My legs were sore, the way I'd feel after a session of heavy weights, but my foot felt good. Good enough, in fact, to wear my three-inch-high-fake-leather-platform shoes all day at work. I relegated the Velcro boot to the back of the closet, promised myself I would up my mileage gradually, and hoped that this might be my last running injury.

Short List of Running Injuries Suffered over the Last 35 Years

1. Broken ankle (tripped on a curb)
2. Achilles tendonitis
3. Shin splints (multiple times)
4. Plantar fasciitis (in both feet, after the Chicago Marathon)
5. Strained calf
6. Irritated hip
7. Sore knees (too many to count)
8. Twisted ankle (at least I didn't break it that time)
9. Concussion (fell and landed face-first)
10. Stress fracture

My foot was healing. My book for Nancy was coming along. I had three chapters in the can and once I incorporated her edits into chapters four and five, those would be done too. The remaining chapters were recipes, which she was working on; when she was done, I'd read through and edit those, write up the citations for the bibliography, and then pull together the entire manuscript, print it out, and read through the entire document in one sitting to proof it and make sure that it hung together. For the latter, I'd need a day of solid, head-down, focused work to get that done and I wasn't sure when I'd have the head space for it.

Working a day job meant there was always a steady torrent of work. While there were times when I wasn't as busy, more often I felt like I had too many assignments piled up, with no sign of stopping. Frank had assigned me two original pieces of content, plus I had six pages to rewrite for another client, several hub pages to write for the SEO team, outlines to revise, and reworks to finish. I worked for three hours Friday morning, banging out a very rough 500-word blog page and starting on another, sneaking in one of the six revisions to break up the writing.

Writing all day was exhausting. My brain was the same orange that got squeezed repeatedly, producing less and less juice until all the squeezing did was exhaust my hand. Freelancing meant that when I finished work for the day, I was done. I could knock off with no sense of guilt or repercussions, and in fact I'd enjoyed that aspect of being self-employed. I was paid for productivity, not time.

Having a job meant that even though I was mentally cooked by 2:00 or 3:00 p.m. or even earlier, I still had to sit at my desk and work, pretend to be working, waste time, all while keeping my anxious monkeys occupied so they didn't pop up with unhelpful thoughts about whether I was making enough money (nope), random pangs of guilt I felt about not working every single minute (even though I rationalized it away with my productivity), or existential angst about whether this was all my life had to offer.

However, while freelancing offered no vacation or sick days, a day job did. I asked for four days of PTO to take the kids to the Wisconsin State Fair and a water park. I'd wanted to take them to New York this summer, but I couldn't swing the money. A mini vacation was better than no vacation at all.

The next morning was one of those days where the minutes crept by. I finished the revision of a bunch of e-com pages for a client that sold bird repellent devices and worked on a couple of new pages for a life settlement broker. I also checked what my estimated social security would be if I started collecting at 62 (unlikely), 67, and 70. If I made it to 67, that meant I had another 14 years to work. Fourteen years! Did I really have to work that long? What if I wanted to change jobs? Who would hire me?

Slow your roll, I reminded myself. You promised yourself you'd stick this job out for a year before you consider anything else. I'd made a solid case for a raise, justifying it in not only the market rate for my position but also my value and the actual bottom line that I had saved the content department. So, why was asking for one making me feel anxious?

Because I wasn't supposed to ask for more. I was supposed to take what was offered and make it work. I didn't want to think about money. I hadn't when I was married. While I had always been motivated to make money, that was to help support our family and to justify my self-employment. If I had a slow month or two, or three, we wouldn't be unable to pay the mortgage or buy groceries. Now, as a single mom, that luxury had disappeared. Money was always the drumbeat in the back of my mind, but I didn't want to actually think about money because thinking about money made me anxious, thinking about how little I made me anxious and irritated, and thinking about how much money I needed to make until my kids were grown and out of the house made me anxious, irritated, and panicky.

The Wednesday before my PTO, Frank made a point of stopping by my desk on his way out. "Have a great vacation!" he said. "Don't think about this place at all."

"Oh, I won't!" I said with a laugh. And I didn't. The kids and I drove to Wisconsin the next day, checked in at the hotel, which included a water park, met my sister, her girlfriend, Shannon, and her daughter, Gabby, at their place and then Ubered to the state fair. We walked around, ate fried foods, went on rides, and watched the pig races. The next morning, we hit the water park and then found a neighborhood bar that had pool tables, and we played pool before capping off the day with more water park action before we crashed for the night. The three of us spent the next day at the water park before meeting my sister for dinner.

I slept better than I had in weeks, waking up to the sensation of being completely rested. The third morning there, I sat on the balcony of the hotel room while the kids lay in bed, occupied with their phones. It was a warm, sunny summer morning, with a slight breeze in the air. My kids were happy. I was making memories with them. I had health insurance. My foot was fine, even after hours of walking up dozens of flights of stairs to the water slides. I embraced all of this goodness, mentally patting myself on the back for spending the money and time to take the trip. For saying yes.

The trip had rebooted my brain, and I was happy to tackle work the next Monday. I already had a plan—to do outlines, catch up on various ancillary tasks, and save any writing assignments for when I worked from home on Tuesday. However, when I'd arrived, I'd found that I had a new priority client that needed outlines for 25 location pages; some were optimizations, which I'd have to add to my list in addition to the outlines. I also had to revise a blog post for the same client, write up my notes from a client kickoff call from last week, and write an e-com brief for another new client. I was starting to feel overwhelmed, but I kept my head down, made steady progress, and left feeling like I'd accomplished a lot.

Until I got home, anyway. I fed the animals and took the puppy around the block before I started editing Nancy's pages. I was about halfway through her recipe chapters, and it was painstaking work, proofreading and formatting each recipe. By the fiftieth time I changed "Cup" to "cup" and "Tablespoon" to "tablespoon," a bell chimed. Way off in the distance. And a thought skittered across my brain … hadn't Nancy said that she had written the recipes according to what the publisher had told her she wanted? Was I formatting them correctly?

I texted her. "Have time for a quick question?"

She called me immediately, and I asked about the capitalizations. "Yeah, I know, it's weird but that's what they want. There is a sheet that lists everything. Didn't I send you that?"

No, she hadn't. But I hadn't asked for it. Or maybe she had, and I'd forgotten. I read through the publisher's style sheet and realized I'd done 43 pages' worth of edits incorrectly. Now, I'd have to go back and redo that work in my so-called spare time.

I could only blame myself. I'd taken this book on, and now I just wanted to be finished with it. School was starting soon, and I still had to take Haley to the doctor for her physical, sign her up for afterschool childcare, send in another copy of Ryan's physical to the high school, get Haley's school supplies, and take them both shopping for clothes. No wonder I felt overwhelmed. I *was* overwhelmed. It had taken less than one day for all of my happy, relaxed, peaceful vacation feelings to dissipate like smoke in the wind.

The Corporate Newbie's Cheat Sheet: Asking for a Raise

First off, don't be afraid to ask. I'm amazed at how many people simply wait, and hope, to be offered a raise. As a freelancer, that never happened. If you wanted more money, whether for an article, a blog post, or even a book, you had to ask for it. So, I got good about asking for more money and often got it.

I'm not saying that you should demand more money six weeks into your new job, but don't be afraid to ask for more, especially if you were hoping for a higher salary at the outset. Be thoughtful and strategic about how you approach this. I suggest you take the following steps:

1. Do your research. Is your salary less than the median for someone in the same position with similar experience? Check out websites like GlassDoor.com, Indeed.com, and the U.S. Bureau of Labor Statistics (www.bls.gov) for data you can use to your advantage.

2. Prove your worth. What have you accomplished so far? Have you saved your department money? Taken on additional responsibilities? Come up with ideas that have helped your department? Don't limit yourself to what you've accomplished so far, but consider what you will be doing in the future, too, and how that will benefit not only your boss but also your department and your company as a whole.

3. Come up with a number. It doesn't hurt to ask for what you want. If you're afraid of asking for too much, or even of asking for too little, consider giving a range. But giving a specific number (that you can show that you're worth) shows that you're serious about getting what you want and should make it more likely for your boss (and possibly his or her boss) to say yes to your request.

4. Consider your approach. This will depend on your boss and your relationship with him or her. If you know your boss prefers face-to-face interaction, schedule a meeting with him or her, and make your pitch. If your boss prefers to communicate electronically, send an email instead (though I think it's smart to ask for an in-person meeting as well). Practice your pitch ahead of time, like you would with any important meeting.

If you get the raise, congrats! If you get turned down, make sure you are given a reason why, and nail down what you can do to make your boss say "yes" the next time you ask.

CHAPTER 8

Disruption

It had been weeks since I'd requested my raise. Finally, one morning Frank emailed, asking me to meet him once I was settled. I grabbed a notebook, pencil, and cup of coffee and walked into Yahoo, trying to downplay my excitement. How much would the raise be?

Frank and I talked dogs for a couple of minutes. Then, he flipped over the piece of paper he had neatly folded in half and folded his hands on the table in front of him. "I've heard from the partners," he said. "They have denied your request for an increase in salary."

I sat there. It didn't register for a minute. "What?"

He continued talking, ticking off the reasons on his list. "You took the job knowing what the salary was," he said. "You've been here less than a year. No one from the content department has had a raise at six months. The partners are willing to consider a raise on your anniversary, on January third.

"There's also no indication that the salary numbers you provided would involve the same kind of work you're doing here," he continued. "And I can say that a company like Digital Edge isn't going to pay a senior copywriter $81,000. We just don't have that pay structure."

"Well, that's ridiculous," I interrupted. "How am I supposed to determine what's a reasonable salary for my position without comparing it to similar jobs at other companies? I have no idea of the pay structure or what I can expect here because we're not allowed to discuss salary per the employee handbook."

Frank didn't say anything, and my temper rose. How many reasons were they going to give me for saying no?

"This … is …. BULLSHIT." I didn't mean to say it. It fell out of my mouth. I shook my head. "This is bullshit," I said again. I thought of how much work I'd done over the last six months and how I'd run with the job, like I'd been encouraged to. I'd expected to get a yes. I'd earned a yes. Instead, I got a no. Not just a no, but a no with seven different reasons. It didn't occur to me to address all of the points I'd enumerated in my formal request. I was too angry. And then, of course, I started to cry. I grabbed a Kleenex and dabbed at my eyes.

"I don't understand this," I said. "This is …. this is wrong."

"I have to say, I didn't like how you phrased part of that letter, saying that you were hired to do content outlines," said Frank. "I made it clear that your job might include some writing. That makes them wonder what I told you about the job."

So, now it was up to me to placate Frank. Really? "That wasn't my intent," I said. "I was trying to show them that I've done far more than what was originally anticipated for this position." I swallowed and willed the tears back into my eyes. "I'm not sure where to go from here."

He uncrossed his arms briefly. "You're, of course, free to look for another position," he said. "Or go back to freelancing."

"I know what my options are, Frank." I took a couple of calming breaths and got my temper under control.

"You're not the only person on the content team who has gone above and beyond," Frank said. "And I have to look out for the team as a whole."

"I get that," I said. "But we're talking about me right now."

"I don't want you to come to work feeling angry or upset," he continued. "Or for this to affect your attitude."

"Do you think I would do that? I'm a professional," I said, steaming. "This isn't going to change how hard I work, how much I do, or the quality of my work, but this feels like they've patted me on the head and told me to go back to work."

"That's another thing. You've mentioned several times that this company is male-dominated and that there aren't many women in management," he said. "All of the project managers are female. And most of the account managers."

"All of the partners are men," I said. "White men," I added. "So, it's male-dominated. Fact, not opinion."

He lifted his hands. "You knew that when you took the job."

"I never said I didn't know that," I said. "But I've been here before. I had a job where I wasn't given a raise for that reason—that they didn't give raises at six months. Then, I found out that other people had gotten raises at six months. They were all men."

Frank started to talk, and I interrupted him. "Hey, I'm not saying that's the case here. I'm just saying I've been in this situation before."

"Again, you're free to look for another job," he said. "You also have more freedom than people who have been here five years."

"That's not compensation or a benefit. It's logistics. What difference does it make if I'm working from the office or working from home?"

"It *is* a benefit," he said. "That flexibility lets you be with your kids. I know there aren't many jobs that offer that."

He was likely wrong on that, but I was tired of arguing. I changed the subject, slightly.

"Is it reasonable for me to expect to be making, say, $55,000 at the end of the year?"

He paused. "That's reasonable."

"But there's no guarantee."

He lifted his hands.

"Right. So, I wait it out, and see."

He nodded. I could feel my temper starting to rise again. "Well, are you okay with me continuing to work from home on Fridays once school starts?" Might as well press my advantage while I had it. He agreed, and I forced myself to remain calm. We talked for a while longer, about the work I was doing for a new client. My face still felt hot. I was embarrassed about crying, but I wasn't going to apologize for it. I was done apologizing. I just wasn't sure what I would do next.

As a freelancer, if I worked for a client who I discovered wasn't worth the money, I became very busy the next time the client reached out with an assignment. Extremely busy. Too busy to take on another assignment. I never burned the proverbial bridge, but I also never worked for a "PIA" (as in pain in the …) twice.

As an employee, though, I didn't have that freedom. I was an adult, and that meant I couldn't simply quit even if I relished the idea. Not with two kids to support, a mortgage, and no idea of who might hire me instead. Yes, I could go back to freelancing, but I'd have to ramp my business back up, which would take time. In weeks, or more likely, months, my miniscule emergency fund would be exhausted by a month or two of no income while I did so.

So, I was stuck, with no option, although I supposed I could walk around sulking at the office, produce low-quality work, and "accidentally" miss some deadlines. I couldn't do that, either. I was going to have to look for another job, one where I could make more money.

I was free to look for another position, as Frank had helpfully pointed out, and that position wasn't simply going to materialize. I would have to go out and find it for the first time in more than 20 years. I had occasionally perused job postings in the past, looking for freelance opportunities, not full-time positions. My gig at Pampered Chef years ago had been the result of a cover letter I'd written seeking freelance work. Now I'd have to look for a position where my experience was an asset, not a liability, where I could grow, and where I'd be appreciated.

It had been almost nine months since I'd proed-and-conned taking the job at Digital Edge. At the time, I'd been blinded by the idea of affordable health insurance, a convenient commute, and steady paychecks and comforted by the fact that I could continue to freelance. Now, I could reflect with more perspective:

Actual Pros (So Far) of Taking the Job

1. Decent, affordable health insurance
2. Regular paychecks
3. Freedom from having to pitch constantly to obtain work
4. Freedom from having to wait on other people (i.e., agents who took weeks to review a proposal or contracts that took months to be reviewed and signed) to obtain steady work
5. The newly discovered ability to work in a corporate environment
6. More structure in my workday
7. A community, albeit somewhat disjointed, at work
8. Notable decrease in anxiety (most of the time, anyway)

9. Significant increase in my understanding of SEO

10. Increase in knowledge about a variety of clients and industries unknown to me before

Good enough. So, what did I want now? I made a new list:

What My Next Job Should Offer

1. More money (which should equate to less day-to-day anxiety, in both the short- and long-term)
2. As much freedom as I currently had (or more)
3. Greater opportunity for advancement
4. Greater opportunity to learn new skills (beyond populating Excel spreadsheets)
5. More appreciation from those I worked with/ sense of being valued by those around me
6. Better benefits (better match on my 401k, more vacation days, you name it)
7. A sense of pride in the company I work for
8. The opportunity to continue to develop my writing skills
9. Working with people who want to connect with other people
10. A sense that my work might be making the world a better place, even in a small way

My list made me realize that I was still smarting from being rejected for a raise. It felt personal. How could it not be? I was asking to be appreciated not only for fulfilling the job requirements but also for what I brought to the position, for being me.

I read through my list again and realized that I had likely described a position that didn't exist. Even if it did, how likely was I to find it? I could job-hunt all I wanted but, in the meantime, I still had to work. I showed up, whether at the office or on my couch, and did my job even when I didn't feel like it. I wrote outlines. I participated in client calls and wrote up notes for them afterward. I wrote pieces of content and revised pieces of content that clients weren't happy with. I scoured job postings, looking for a position that matched most of the requirements on my new list, or at least appeared to. I had time to do that now; I'd finished Nancy's book the week before.

I'd written a book—albeit a short one—in four months while working full time and parenting (though often doing a subpar job of that, it felt like). I'd managed to harness both sides of my freelance brain to do so. I had my creative brain, which did the thinking, conceptualizing, and writing, and my boss brain, which forced the creative brain (often balky, unmotivated, and sluggish) to get the … work … done. The Boss couldn't always force Creative to deliver but applied steady (not necessarily gentle) pressure throughout the process.

Now I could turn both brains off for a while. Since I'd started working at Digital Edge, I'd written more than a dozen articles for freelance clients, including *Chicago Health*, a local health publication and *NextAvenue.org*, a website for people 50+. I'd written the draft of Nancy's book. I'd done all this while holding a full-time job.

For the first time since I'd started the job, I had no freelance deadlines, no assignments that needed to be turned around, no interviews to line up, and no research to conduct. For the coming days I would be a "normal" employee—one with one job. The kickoff calls were keeping me busy and giving me a window into the big picture that I had lacked before. I received invitations to the kickoff calls from the AMs and planned my days around them. The salesman would typically kick off the call, introducing the DE team, and then the AM would take over. I'd listen and take notes as the AM walked the client through what to expect in the coming months of the campaign. The AM would introduce me at some point, and I'd ask a couple of questions specific to content and then thank the client and AM, put my phone back on mute, and stay on the call in case the client mentioned anything else relevant.

Some clients were already fairly savvy about SEO, were already tracking conversion and traffic numbers, and had specific goals, like increasing the number of leads from 30 a month to 100 or more. Others, typically smaller companies, were newer to SEO and often needed spoon-feeding. After every call, I reviewed my notes, determined what was relevant, and then pulled the notes together into a brief memo that included background on the client, what it sold and what its goals were, along with information that might be helpful for the content team.

For example, one client, a med spa in Florida, performed a lot of Botox. While Botox itself was not a big income generator for the client, it was a big traffic generator, and the owner wanted to figure out how to cross-sell other services (like Juvéderm, photo facials, and CoolSculpting) to patients. She also felt that the tone of the site was too conversational and wanted a more professional, credentialed voice. Another client, which sold kefir, a fermented dairy beverage, mentioned the importance of being careful when making health claims unless there was empirical evidence to back them up. You could use a phrase like "may help improve digestive function" but not "improves digestive function" unless you had studies to prove that. Another client, a local moving company, wants to stay away from keywords that included *cheap* and *affordable*.

This was the kind of information that could help Melissa and me write more effective outlines as well as help our writers deliver content that was more likely to please the client. After participating in the first couple of calls, I realized that the content team wasn't the only department of Digital Edge that could benefit from them. Anyone who worked on the client's campaign might find them helpful. I used our CMS program to identify each of the team members who had been assigned to the client and started cc-ing them on the emails I sent to Frank.

The new increase in workload meant that I hadn't had as much time to look for a new job as I'd expected. I checked the job listings nearly daily and had applied for a half-dozen positions, all of which were within a ten-mile radius as I wasn't willing to commute into Chicago, where most of the promising positions were. Some positions were a stretch in terms of my experience, but applying for them made me feel more in control of my destiny. Even if I didn't get a new job immediately, I was letting the universe know I was open to other possibilities. That was my freelance mindset reasserting itself, or at least trying to, even as I slid deeper into my employee identity.

I had a real job now, one that I wasn't thinking of as a respite from freelancing but as reality. The reality was that I wasn't a unique snowflake. I was like everyone else, a wage worker, an indentured servant who worked for money, focused more on keeping my job more than reaching for what might be next, and more focused on not losing my job than on worrying about whether I was happy there. That had taken nearly eight months.

Not that every day of freelancing was a cakewalk. Every year or so, I'd have a career crisis, usually brought on by a surfeit of work, a sense of meaninglessness, or the fear that I couldn't do this for the rest of my life, and I reconsidered what I was doing. Every time I'd found that the benefits (freedom to set my own hours, the ability to choose the kind of work I did, the satisfaction of distilling facts and information into a never-before-existing article or entire book, and the pride I took in what I did) had outweighed the drawbacks (slow-paying clients, slowdowns in work, losing out on projects I wanted, an ever-present anxiety from needing to drum up work when I wasn't busy). Every time.

Until this job had come along with its sexy health insurance. I had wanted an adventure. I'd wanted to try something else. And I had. Now I could feel the shift on an internal level. I was shape shifting. It felt like the very molecules that made up Kelly were being rearranged, reordered, and reconstituted. I was starting to wonder if I could go back to freelancing after a year. I was still straddling the divide between employee and ghostwriter/freelancer, and now I wasn't sure which one would win.

The Corporate Newbie's Cheat Sheet: Deciding Whether to Look for a New Job (and Why You Should)

Thinking of looking for a new job? Congratulations! And if not, you should be.

I don't mean that you should be actively devoting hours of your day to searching for a new position if you're content with the one you have. I do mean that you should be keeping tabs on companies that you're interested in, what your colleagues are doing, and whether an opportunity might develop someplace else.

As Alec Baldwin's character in Glengarry Glen Ross said, "always be closing."

What you don't want is to realize you wanted a different job like, well, yesterday, and you're still trapped in the same place because your resume is woefully outdated, you have no sense of what the job market looks like, especially for positions in your particular industry, you're burned out and maybe even bitter, and now you're supposed to shine your best self out into the universe.

So, be smart, with an up-to-date resume ready to go in case you do hear of an opportunity that may be a good fit. Say, you apply for a different job, get an offer, and have to decide whether to stay or go? That's a much better conundrum than realizing you're trapped with few, if any, alternatives.

CHAPTER 9

Alignment

Between kickoff calls, writing up notes afterward, and writing tasks, I was spending less time writing outlines while Melissa had picked up the slack. She'd started working from home one day a week, which meant that she and I only saw each other on Mondays. We'd catch up, chatting during our day, and sometimes I'd book a meeting in Yahoo where we'd talk, ostensibly about work. I'd told her that I'd started looking for another job.

"I've made a lot of mistakes here already," I said. "I've said too much, stepped on Frank's toes too many times, and almost gotten fired twice. I feel like all I do is apologize." I sighed. "Of course, that's an FMS." I'd shared my Frank Management Strategies with Sarah and later with Melissa. FMS included emailing Frank before or at 8:00 a.m. on the mornings I worked from home, so he'd know I was at my desk, so to speak, asking permission to do anything outside of the ordinary as far as work went, keeping him updated on what I was working on, and yes, apologizing on the regular (though that was getting harder and harder to do.)

"What about you? What's your plan? Do you have a plan?"

She sipped her water. "I don't know. I guess I don't have one yet."

"Well, I don't have one, either, other than looking for another job and trying not to get fired, which is not much of a plan." I drank more of my tea. I'd started limiting myself to two cups of coffee a day, switching to herbal tea afterward. It made my afternoons drag, but I had an easier time falling asleep if I avoided caffeine after late morning. "What about that email from last week?"

We'd received an email from one of the partners informing the company that management had made some changes, which included the fact that four employees were no longer employed by Digital Edge. The email was brief and emotionless and gave no indication of what had happened, or why.

"Yeah, that was weird."

"It makes me paranoid," I admitted. "Or even more paranoid! I keep thinking maybe they're getting rid of squeaky wheels. And, well, if that's the case," I pointed at myself. "You know, 'squeak, squeak.'"

Melissa burst out laughing, and I did, too. "Geez, I hope you're learning something from me. Don't do what I did! Keep your head down, keep to yourself, do your job, go home." I shrugged. "Although apparently that is impossible for me."

I had mentored Melissa as well as I could, trying to be the boss that I wish I'd had when I was in my 20s or, hell, the boss I wish I had now. I had never had a mentor as a lawyer, but as a freelancer, I looked for them. I'd paid attention to writers who were further along in their careers than I was, especially the female ones, and tried to emulate then. Many had been generous with advice and hard-earned freelance smarts. I soaked up everything I could and then in turn shared that with other writers. My freelance career had been built around the pillars of mindset, efficiency, and connections, and I had taken a similar approach with my job. I took it seriously; I was willing to learn and to admit when I was wrong (and, of course, apologize). I looked for ways to work as quickly as I could without sacrificing quality. I tried to create relationships with people, and if I couldn't do that, I treated them with respect.

My freelance pillars, however, were not quite as effective in a corporate environment. My mindset didn't appear to matter as long as I got my work done. My efficiency hadn't been rewarded, at least not yet. After all, I was making the same salary as I had when I'd started. Regardless of how much work I accomplished, there was always more work waiting, so my typical freelance carrots were rendered useless. I no longer took myself out to lunch on a Friday afternoon after a busy week and then spent the rest of the afternoon reading on the couch because I had accomplished every task on my to-do list. I worked the same 40 hours, regardless.

As for connections? I hadn't built many of those, either. I was still figuring out the corporate hierarchy, but the nature of the company meant that the departments rarely worked together. Through the kickoff calls, I'd gotten to know some of the account managers better, and I liked all the project managers, all of whom were women. I talked with the sales guys and SEO guys regularly, but other than Melissa and Sarah, there was no one I would call an actual work friend. I'd expected more of a community at work, but I also realized my expectations tended to be too high of everything and everyone.

I told Melissa I hadn't heard anything about any of the jobs I'd applied for. That in itself was frustrating. I'd spent an hour or two crafting a cover letter for each position I'd been interested in, reconfiguring the template of my resume to better match the skills required. Other than the formular "we-have-received-your-resume" email response for each job, however, I'd heard nothing.

"I don't know," I said to Melissa. "Even if I get a different job, what's to say it won't be even worse than working here?" I leaned back in my chair. "And I won't be able to work with you, and we won't be able to have these important work-related meetings in Yahoo." I picked up my notebook. "Don't worry, I'm probably going nowhere."

I meant that in every sense of the phrase. The more writing and kickoff calls I did, the more I realized that I didn't want to do outlines anymore. A lot of it was boring, busy work. I tried to reframe. I did like the kickoff calls, talking to clients, and getting a handle on what they were looking for content-wise. I liked writing, and I liked revising content even more because I could nearly always improve the raw material. I also liked talking to the SEO guys about strategy, brainstorming, and coming up with ideas for blog pages for clients.

Reframed, the job wasn't that awful. So, what was dragging me down? The worry that I was transforming, even against my will, from a freelancer to a (sigh) employee. The realization that I had another 13 or 14 years of work ahead of me. The frustration of making so little for the quality and sheer quantity of work I was producing. The fear that if I went somewhere else, it could conceivably be worse. The fear that I couldn't get another job. The fear that I was settling. I *was* settling every day I showed up and remained part of the machine.

I stowed away these thoughts but revisited them Saturday night with Gabriel. I hadn't spoken to him much the last couple of months, but we still texted occasionally or caught up when we had time. If he walked by the house with his dog, I'd send him a text that read, "Wow, a super-sexy guy just walked by my house." Then, I'd add, "And then you came by." It always made me laugh, even if he read it and then gave me the finger over his shoulder.

I told him about my suspected metamorphosis and how it worried me. "It's like the best parts of me are the freelance parts! I feel like they are disappearing. It's like that Star Trek episode with the Borg. I am being assimilated," I said.

He got it immediately. "I was afraid that would happen," he said.

"What do you mean?"

"We're wired by nature to be self-sufficient," Gabriel said. "All employees chafe under the yoke of employment."

"I disagree! That's the whole metamorphosis that I'm talking about. As you morph into an employee, that sense of independence and drive disappears, or mostly disappears," I said, trying to find the positive in my predicament. "You accept your lot. You work for a paycheck and look for other ways to find pleasure and meaning in life: hobbies. Friends. Family. Netflix shows." I found myself trailing off now that I was forced to defend my position.

As a freelancer, a tremendous amount of my identity and self-esteem had stemmed from work. I not only liked what I did but also was pretty good at it, good enough to make a decent living in a field where many people couldn't. That fact was not only part of who I was but also something I was proud of. As I let go of my identity as a freelancer and the pride that accompanied it, I also recognized my job wouldn't fill that gap. I needed more than Netflix for that.

Where did Walt fit into this picture? I wasn't sure. We continued to see each other on weekends, hang out, have (still very good) sex, play pool on Saturday nights, and then do the crossword on Sunday mornings. We returned to our separate residences and our usual lives at the end of every weekend. I wasn't satisfied with it, but I wasn't willing to walk away from him, either.

Humans are more conditioned to avoid pain than to seek pleasure, and making any kind of significant life change required an enormous amount of energy, drive, and commitment. The bigger the change, the greater the energy. Take getting divorced. You don't just wake up one morning and get divorced. You might decide to get divorced, but then you had to see that decision through (unless you'd already changed your mind, again, and decided to make things work.) You had to keep on getting divorced, day after day. You had to keep getting divorced while you hired a lawyer, keep getting divorced as you starting splitting up your possessions, keep getting divorced as you realized how much money you were walking away from, keep getting divorced as you told your kids, keep getting divorced as you lay in bed and worried that you were doing your kids irreparable harm, keep getting divorced as you looked for a place to live, and keep getting divorced as you had to tell people. It went on and on. It takes months to get divorced, and by the time you are divorced, you've spent such an inordinate amount of energy you're now just a hollowed-out shell of a person figuring out how to put her life back together and make sure that her kids are going to be okay. In the back of your head, you occasionally doubt yourself and think, why couldn't you just suck it up and stay married, but you refuse to listen to that voice and keep getting divorced. Then one day, you are. Another day, you realize you're used to it. Then one day, you realize that you're happier than you have been in years. People see that and have no idea of what you went through to go from married to divorced. They think it was easy.

Three years later, I didn't regret getting divorced. I regretted waiting so long to do so; I regretted not saving more money; I regretted being talking into buying a too-large, overly expensive house that we hadn't needed and had had to sell after the divorce. I didn't regret being married, though, because without the marriage, we wouldn't have Ryan and Haley.

Erik and I could sit together at sporting events, talk about the kids, and coparent well together, but the passion I'd felt for him and for our life as a family had burned out long ago. Sometimes, I looked at him and thought, I used to be madly in love with this person. His happiness and our marriage was my first priority for years, for almost a decade until Ryan came along. Ryan trumped everything, including Erik, and I discovered that Erik didn't have the bandwidth to be a husband and a dad. He grew increasingly resentful and distant, and I grew increasingly unhappy and kept lowering my expectations until they were subterranean, Then, my dad died, and Erik didn't come with me to my parents' house. I asked him to, begged him to a few days later, after I'd spent days taking care of my mom and calling family and friends and making arrangements and trying not to have an anxiety attack. He still didn't come, and I realized this was what I was settling for: someone who couldn't show up for me or wasn't willing to. I realized I didn't want to settle, or try, anymore. Could I have tried harder? Could I have stuck it out? Should have I have settled? Maybe. But I didn't want to swim around in a miasma of whats-ifs, so I reframed, as usual, and focused on the positive.

I'd read recently that as you grow and learn, you are capable of making changes that may have been impossible, even unthinkable, before. With new information and new experience, you can make a choice—a better, healthier choice—than you may have made years, even months or weeks earlier. In other words, you are not doomed to repeat the same patterns of your past, no matter how entrenched they seem to be.

That resonated with me. I knew that you never walk in the same stream twice. Even if it felt like the same stream, you weren't the same person at the end. When I'd written novels, I was aware that at the end of writing the book, I was a different person. The challenge was keeping the novel consistent, even though the writer had changed and grown. I recognized that the person I would be at the end of the year wouldn't be the same person I'd been before.

What did I want for her? I wanted her to be not just older but smarter, more secure, calmer, more confident, more at home in her body, more comfortable in her skin even though that skin had another year of sun damage, gravity, and stress placed on it. Let's admit it, couldn't she magically be 10, okay 15, pounds thinner, too?

That wasn't likely, as I wasn't willing to dial back eating crap during the day or a glass or two of wine several nights a week, but I was working on the security part. I'd been setting aside 10 percent of my income in my 401k at work, but that was the extent of my retirement planning. I knew I needed to save more, but how much more? In an SEP? A Roth? Should I buy stocks, bonds, or mutual funds? I knew that index funds traded less frequently and were a better all-over bet, at least according to Gabriel and a book he'd told me to read on the subject, but I was having trouble acting. I couldn't have analysis paralysis because I hadn't even analyzed my options yet—I had far too many of them and knew that the more options I had, the less likely I would be to make a decision.

I was spending $400/month for Edward Jones to "manage" my money and had been for at least 15 years. "Management," as best I could tell, meant that I met with my Edward Jones rep, whom I genuinely liked, once a year or so, talked vaguely about my vague goals, and then scheduled another meeting 12 months out. I had the illusion that my financial future wasn't completely in my (pretty much completely incapable) hands, so I had stayed with Edward Jones until a few weeks ago.

I'd finally taken the step of moving my money from Edward Jones to Vanguard index funds, where I would be paying much lower fees—about $400/year instead of $400/ month. I'd talked to Gabriel about it last December and had set up the account then but hadn't been transferred the money over to fund it. With Monica, my Edward Jones representative, I felt a little safer. Or at least not quite so alone.

I explained my reasoning to Gabriel when I admitted that I hadn't yet moved my very small retirement fund over to Vanguard.

"So, what are you paying a month to Edward Jones?"

"Ummm … about $400 a month." I almost whispered it.

"You're paying $400 a month to not feel alone?" Gabriel said. "Pay me $200 a month, and I'll make you feel not alone."

"Shut up," I said. "You should do that for free."

He was doing math. "Kelly, if you're paying $400 a month over the next 20 years that's going to cost you a quarter of a million dollars."

"Okay! Okay! Okay! I hear you. You're making me anxious." I had to get off of the phone for a client call. Afterward, I took the dog around the block, thinking about what he'd said and why I hadn't moved my money. It came down to fear. I was afraid. And having my money at Edward Jones made me feel less afraid, but all I'd done was meet with my advisor once a year to talk about my mutual funds and my far-off retirement goals. She hadn't advised me during the year about what to buy, what to sell, or how to make money when the market was hot. She hadn't actually made any money for me (thanks in large part to the fees), and she hadn't actually lessened the fear that I would outlive my money (which now seemed more and more possible, thanks to my recent obsessive calculations of what I should have saved for retirement by now).

What if I moved my money, the stock market took a huge dump, and I lost everything and had nothing for retirement? Then I would have to work … possibly forever. I'd have to live off of Social Security and whatever I could make in the meantime. Maybe live in one of my kids' basements. That wasn't appealing, though the idea of them living forever in mine was even less so. I walked, took deep breaths, and accepted that I had no control over any of this. I only had the illusion of control. I would have to deal with a stock market dump if and when it happened. When I got home, I found the link to transfer my account and started the online paperwork process to actually move my money over.

Gabriel had already told me which index funds to put the money in, but he surprised me with a spreadsheet he'd created on a zip drive. "Here you go," he said. I hadn't realized what he had done until I opened it up on my Mac. He'd put in the formulas so I would know how to allocate my money through four different index funds to start and listed the ones he recommended. I'd completed the paperwork, mailed it in, and allocated the money into the relevant accounts once it had been transferred. It had taken me nearly a year to finalize the process, but I'd done it.

Walt didn't understand what a significant move this was for me. He'd been staying at my house more often and working on jobs in the western suburbs that were much closer to my house than his. My house had become his convenient extended-stay hotel. It had been strange going from seeing each other for a 24-hour weekend to having him here day after day. I liked it.

We'd argued on Saturday night, though. I'd had a couple of glasses of wine and had brought up the fact that we hadn't taken a trip together in more than a year, even though he'd taken a week in June to go to Vegas with his friend Mike and another eight days to go to Arizona with him to golf.

The argument had devolved, as arguments do. He asserted, not for the first time, that I didn't like going to his house and that I rarely visited him.

This time, thought, I didn't argue. "That's true," I said. "You're right. I'd rather be at my house."

We talked about it for a while. "I don't want to just sit on the couch at your house and do nothing except watch TV," I said.

"That's what I do sometimes. Why can't you just come over and do that when that's what I want to do?"

Because it's boring, I thought. And I don't want to. And I'm selfish. I want things my way, all of the time. I'd rather be at my house. Because, well, it's my house.

"I'd just be sitting there. Probably reading a book," I said.

"Fine. Whatever you want."

He did want me there, even if he didn't show me. "I love having you here," I'd tell him when we were lying in bed. I'd lean over and kiss him when I was getting up from the couch or squeeze his neck when we were driving in his truck. I showed him all the time that I loved him. Why couldn't he do the same? I recognized that I wanted and needed more from him than he did from me, and that made me feel unwanted, needy, and desperate. Instead of talking to him about it, though, I waited and asked the universe to work things out for me. I had enough on my plate, with at least nine years of heavy lifting to do with the kids.

It was the time in my parenting life to be stable, consistent, and present and to teach them what they would have to know eventually—like how to put gas in your car, do laundry, balance your checkbook, manage your money, cook a reasonably healthy meal, spend less than you made, get along with people you didn't particularly like, and manage your stress in hopefully healthy ways, things that I myself wasn't all that great at, actually. Still, that was my responsibility.

What could I do? Be both harder and easier on myself. Harder when it came to things like being more present with my kids. Easier when it came to the fact that I was doing a decent job. I wanted to have more fun with them, I realized. Freelancing on top of my job hadn't just sapped me. It had sapped my energy and my desire to connect with them. The realization was sobering and sad.

So, what next? To take the small steps. I taught Haley how to play gin rummy and she picked it up quickly, beating me four hands out of four the second night we played. I took Ryan to the driving range to hit balls with me. I made sure we sat down for dinner even if we were eating takeout from Panda because I'd realized that cooking dinner every night was an unrealistic pressure on me. I focused on the smallest things, liked Haley calling out, "I love you a little less each day, Mom!" (her take on "I love you a tiny, tiny bit") one night after I'd put her to bed.

While my life at home was picking up, work was slow, very slow, which made Frank's recent email to the entire department worrisome. He'd said that Sean had asked him to fill out a spreadsheet with the content team's hours. "Your hours are 7-3:30 on Monday/Wednesday and 8-4:30 on Tu/Thur/Fri, correct?" Yes, that was correct. And, um, why do you want to know? Why did Sean want to know? What was going on?

Sarah and I talked about it while I walked Jet on my lunch break. She was working from home five days a week now, and while I missed her at the office, we'd gotten in the habit of texting regularly and talking every few days. "We are really slow," I said. "Like the slowest we've ever been. SEO is so behind, I don't know when we're going to catch up."

The next morning, Melissa and I sat in Yahoo and talked it over. "I could finish everything on my plate right now in like 20 minutes," I said. "What about you?"

"Same."

"Crap." I shook my head. "This thing with asking about our hours? We're not nearly as productive as we were months ago. The content team has doubled in size in the last eight months, and now we're not busy enough to justify it." Besides Melissa, Sarah, and me, we now had a new writer, Anne, who sat behind Sarah, on the team.

"I have to say, I'm a little anxious," I admitted to Melissa. "Technically, Anne is the latest hired, but I'm sure I make more money than you and she do." That was obvious, wasn't it? Not a violation of company policy? Melissa could do my job, and I knew it. No one other than Frank had an idea of what I did for the company, and Frank and I hadn't spoken— other than to say the briefest remarks like, "good morning or "you'll have that piece of content later today"— since our meeting more than two months ago.

People could be, and had been, let go with no warning whatsoever, and I had given Frank ample reason to can my ass. Any security I felt like I may have had was disappearing faster than the Friday morning donuts in the nook, especially considering that I had little work to do.

I stretched out the last two optimizations assigned to me and wrote the last 20 outlines on my list at glacial pace. Even so, I was completely caught up on work with an hour to go before the day ended.

What was I going to say if Frank asked me what I was working on? "Um, nothing" seemed like a good way to get fired, especially if the company was cutting staff. I sent a chirpy email telling him that a major client was supposed to have keyword approval soon (25 outlines! Yay!) and that I welcomed writing assignments.

Not that my writing was improving. I had become more creative about working keywords into resistant content, but the focus was on keywords, not quality. I found myself writing to word count more and more often, deliberately choosing convoluted, wordy phrases that would get me closer to the current Google ideal of 450 instead of writing the lean copy I preferred.

I'd said the same to Sarah a few days before, when she came over on a Friday afternoon after work. "I know! It's all piecework, and piecework by its nature is not quality work," she agreed. She'd asked Frank about the possibility about going part-time and had been shot down with a terse email that concluded with him telling her if she wasn't interested in working 40 hours/week, to let him know ASAP.

"I hate that the focus is on quantity, not quality," I said. "Plus, I get almost no feedback on the work I do. I feel like I'm working in the dark." I sighed, rubbing Jetty with my foot. She was lying on the floor happily gnawing on a giant chew toy.

"It's not even piecework," said Sarah. "It's like working at a factory. You're just producing the same thing over and over, with no regard to quality. It's stifling." Sarah's job was even worse than mine, editing 8-12 pieces of content a day. All day. Every day.

"I feel like Frank doesn't even like me," added Sarah.

"Same. But does he like anyone?" I cackled.

"I have ideas I want to pursue, and I have a ticking clock," said Sarah. "I don't know that this is worth it to me anymore."

"I get it," I said. "At the same time, I don't want to get

fired. I also don't want to take another job just to take another job. It has to be more money and more opportunity."

"I've been thinking about it, and I think it's possible for you to make Digital Edge work for you," said Sarah.

I waved my hand. "Let's table that for now. What about you? I know you have a variety of reasons for leaving," I said. "Which one is the main one?" I got up to use the bathroom. "You've got to two minutes to figure it out." I came back and resettled myself on the couch, looking at her expectantly.

"It's not what I want to do," said Sarah, ticking off the reasons on her hand. "I took the job because I wanted connection and community, and I don't have that. I'm bored senseless doing the same things day after day. I have work I want to do for myself, essays I want to write." She continued and told me she wanted to start readers' and writers' groups. "Something I can carry into retirement," she added.

I realized it was only a matter of time before Sarah left, and she was the only real friend I'd made at DE. When she left, who would I be able to talk about work? My freelance friends didn't get it. There was Melissa, of course, but she was at the nascency of her career. She hadn't amassed the experience to be bitter or at least world-wise. Sarah was smart and seasoned. She was a parent, though her kids were grown, and she had a vocabulary as big as mine. I could talk books and writing with her. I loved the chance to get all my big words out and show them off.

That was one reason I'd asked Raechell out. She was one of the project managers in her early 30s, and we'd spoken a few times. She was warm, open, and talkative, and I'd learned she had a side business creating and selling essential oil products. That had led to a discussion about side hustles, and I'd been intrigued by the fact she had another business in addition to her day job. We'd met for drinks at Cadence, the only bar I frequented.

"I've been at Digital Edge more than nine months," I said, as we arranged ourselves at the bar. "Shouldn't I be having a work baby by now?" I joked. I asked how long she'd been there and was shocked at her answer.

"Eleven years? Holy cow! Why have you been here so long? Have you ever thought about leaving? Do you really like your job? You like what you do? Or is inertia?" After all, inertia governed most decisions whether people realized it or not. Every day I was finding it easier to stay the course I was on—to continue working for Digital Edge, to continue dating Walt—than to change. Inertia governed more than the rules of motion. It governed human behavior as well.

"When I started, there were only seven or eight of us," said Raechell. "We went to lunch together. We hung out together. We were like a family." Since then, the company had grown to ten times that size, and she had stayed on, starting out as a designer before she moved into her current position as a project manager. She liked working with clients directly but missed doing design work. Overall, though, she was happy here.

I filled her in, a bit, on the rejection of my raise, what I liked about the company, and what I didn't. "I actually like working here," I said. "I like the people I work with, but I'm starting to feel like there may not be a place for me. If that's the case, it doesn't make sense for me to stay."

Raechell nodded and listened. We talked for a while, and our talk ranged from work to side gigs to relationships to what we wanted to do with our lives. My favorite types of conversational topics. She asked about my writing, and after swearing her to secrecy, I admitted that I was writing a book.

"I'm calling it *The Book That Got Me Fired*," I said, laughing. "I probably need a different title."

"You can't change the name! That's a great name!"

"Well, I still don't know what it's about," I said. "I thought it was going to be about working with Millennials, but it's actually turning out to be about anxiety, identity, connection, and meaning." I drank some of my wine. "I know too much when it comes to publishing. I need to have social media numbers, Insta followers, and a platform, and I don't have that."

"You think too much," she said.

"Well, yeah, thanks, Captain Obvious," I replied.

"You do. You need to stop overthinking it."

That was true. I just needed to write the damn book and figure out next steps later on.

"I'm going to say something else. I'm sorry if it's too direct, but whenever you talk about Walt, you always say, 'he is not my guy.'"

"I do?" Apparently my indecision was more obvious than I realized.

"So, if he's not your guy, what are you doing?" she asked. "If you have something in that bucket, the universe won't put anything else in that bucket."

I nodded, thinking, I find someone else who believes in the universe, and what happens? She tells me things I don't want to hear. The fact was that I'd been leaving too much up to the universe. There were just over two months before the end of the year, and I needed to take action. I'd been applying for jobs but had yet to receive anything more than a canned email response. What if I didn't get another job? What if I couldn't? Maybe I should listen to Sarah and figure out a way to make Digital Edge work for me. That meant reframing, a skill I was good at. I did have a certain amount of freedom in how I managed my time. I did work from home three days a week. I did like most of the people I worked with. On the other hand, I needed more money, and I had finally figured out that my future, at least at Digital Edge, wasn't in my hands anymore. It was in Frank's.

The partners relied on the department managers to determine raises, promotions, and terminations. Digital Edge staff didn't try to circumvent the company hierarchy; they relied on their managers. I needed to do the same. I decided to talk to Frank, asking for his advice and guidance. Doing so was strategic. What I really wanted to ask was, "How do I guarantee that I get the raise I need at the end of the year?" Talking about money, however, made Frank defensive. So, I was going to couch it in asking for help, leadership, support, and appealing to his alpha male brain. He had daughters, after all.

Gabriel had been right months ago, when he'd said I was in a relationship with Frank, even if it wasn't a romantic one. I'd given lip service to the idea of managing the relationship, but instead I'd ignored it because I didn't know how to fix it. Part of me wanted to say, "Do you just not like me anymore?" That was so girl. It didn't matter if he liked me, I reminded myself. I was certain that he was routinely threatened, annoyed, and irritated by me. That didn't bode well for a raise or for my future.

While the raise might be my goal, a good working relationship with my boss was the gateway to it. As a freelancer, I'd been able to jettison clients I didn't like working with. That wasn't possible at Digital Edge or at any other job. As an employee, I'd have to make it work.

I planned for the meeting, writing down my goals:

1. Make it as likely as possible to get "my" raise at year's end.

2. Determine what I could do, if anything, to attract positive attention from the partners/purse-string-holders (other than going directly to them, which hadn't proven particularly fruitful before).
3. Reconnect with Frank and thaw a little bit of the frozen tundra that existed between us.
4. Let Frank know I cared about my job and wanted to continue to work at Digital Edge.

Next up, figuring out what to say, in what order, and how.

The Corporate Newbie's Cheat Sheet: Getting a Handle on Your Finances

Let's talk money for a minute.

(You got uncomfortable there, right? It's okay. Take a deep breath, and stay with me.)

People make plenty of mistakes with their money. They spend too much. They save too little. They underestimate what they'll need in retirement and overestimate their ability to stay on a budget. I can't address all of these issues in a few brief paragraphs.

All I want you to do is take a more proactive approach to your money, in particular your savings for retirement because you're working not only to pay for your day-to-day expenses but also for the future. If you have kids at home, you're probably saving at least a little for college, but you should be stashing money for *your* future, too—at least 10 percent of your income.

If you're not already saving that with your company's 401(k), set that up now. Company doesn't offer a 401(k)? Set up an IRA. If you have zero clue about how to manage your money, consider using a company like Edward Jones to help you do so or talk to a savvy financial friend and get started on your own. Check out websites like www.betterInvesting.org and www.fool.com to get a handle on the basics.

I still don't know that much about investing, but I do know that index funds are usually a smart investment and carry lower fees than other types of investments. I also understand the time value of money, which means the earlier you invest, the better.

I wish I would have invested far more money earlier in adulthood, but I didn't. That fact does make me anxious as I worry about whether I can save enough for retirement. I am doing what I reasonably can now, and that helps. I strongly encourage you to do the same.

CHAPTER 10

Mitigation

My planning and forethought worked.

Not only did I survive the meeting with Frank, it went well. I'd decided in advance not to bring up anything that might make him defensive. He sat across from me, his arms folded across his chest.

I started by talking about some procedural matters about e-com clients before easing into the rest of the conversation. "At this point, I've done more than 30 kickoff calls," I said. "I wondered if you have any feedback for me, what you thought of the notes, or if there's anything you want me to include or not include, that kind of thing. I'm erring on the side of including information unless I think it's completely irrelevant."

"The notes look great," said Frank. "But at this point, it's too small of a sample size to see if this has value in terms of content and whether it's having an impact on how happy clients are or whether they're making revision requests."

"I agree that the sample size is too small, and also it hasn't been long enough to measure the results," I said, working on building a bridge between the two of us. "I do think it's worthwhile to have me on the calls. I'm hoping we'll have proof of that in some tangible way soon."

Was I thawing the tundra? Who knew? I continued on. "So, I'd also appreciate your help and guidance. My annual review is less than two months away. What would you suggest

I do to help communicate my value to the people who hold the purse strings?"

Frank crossed his leg over his knee and adjusted his sweater before recrossing his arms. He reminded me that when it came to salaries, he didn't have much authority, but that he could make a case for employees deserving more than what they had been budgeted for. The way he described it, it came down to spreadsheets and budget numbers. I know knew that our department would have a dollar figure assigned to it, with salaries making up the majority of it, and that there wouldn't be a lot of play with those figures.

"Roger deserves to be paid a lot more than he's making," Frank said. It wasn't the first time he'd said this, and I agreed that that was likely true (though I had no way of knowing what Roger made, except that if he was working for this company, "not a lot" came to mind). Once again, I pictured a pie. You're dividing it eight (or nine, or ten) different ways. The more ways you have to split the pie, the smaller your piece would be.

Wait, wait. It could be a bigger pie! Still, I doubted that. The bottom line was that if someone in my department made more money, there would probably be less money (or less pie) for me. So, we were in fact competing against each other for the same pie. Just how much pie there was remained to be seen, but I told Frank I planned to formally request a raise once again. "I recognize that you already know what I've done here, but it's important to me that I demonstrate my value to the partners," I said. "I want to make it easy for them to say yes."

Frank nodded. "Do what you need to," he said. "I'll pass it along."

A week or so later, one of the AMs asked me to participate in a call with a client who wasn't happy with the content we'd produced for her. The AM used the word *escalating*, and she the AM and I managed to tag-team the client into submission. Now, it was up to me to rewrite the content and make the client happy.

I asked Frank's permission to do so. He had forwarded an email he'd sent to some of the higher-ups, making it clear that I wasn't to be asked to participate in these kinds of content calls without asking him for permission first. Was I now a stud pony? Poor analogies aside, I knew that his frustration had more to do with the slights he'd experienced (either real or perceived— did it matter?) and that I was simply a lightning rod for some of this anger. I didn't know how to manage it, other than assuring him that I was encouraging DE team members to follow protocol.

I wasn't sure if he was threatened by me or threatened by other team members wanting to work with me. Most likely both. But at least he wasn't blaming me for what was happening, and that was what I needed to be able to progress and thrive.

I felt more content at home, too. I'd run/walked three or four days a week the last couple of weeks, and my foot was okay. The kids were doing fine. I was caught up on freelance work, save for one assignment for *Next Avenue*, and I'd finished the research for it. I needed about an hour to pull the story together—if I was in the mood. If not, it would take me several hours to produce the same result.

That was something I knew from years of freelancing. Strike when my brain was in writing mode, and I could bang out work—good, solid work— with minimal effort. When I wasn't feeling it, though, I could spend hours moving words around with little to show for it. As an employee, though, we had less (or rather, no) ability to ride those waves of productivity and focus. I had already learned that I couldn't work eight hours a day. It simply wasn't possible, and I didn't think anyone else was doing it, either. We remained hamstrung by the eight-hour day and the 40-hour-week. When I worked from home, I did chores during my workday. I walked the dog, threw in a load of laundry, swung by the store, and ran Haley to dance class or Ryan to basketball practice during my work hours. I felt a little guilty but reminded myself that I didn't work a full eight-hour day at work. I killed plenty of time on Facebook and Dlisted and lately had been using online calculators to stress myself out about how little I had saved for retirement.

Yet, I still wasn't willing to forgo adventures and had bought tickets to see Jim Gaffigan, a comedian we both liked, as a surprise for Walt. Gaffigan was playing in downtown Chicago, and I'd suggested that we stay at a hotel that night and make a short weekend of it. He wasn't willing to spend the money, and the discussion devolved into an argument.

Stand-up Comedians I've Seen in Person

1. Jim Breuer
2. Gallagher (at a state fair, no less)
3. Dane Cook (multiple times)
4. Kathy Griffin
5. Stephen Lynch
6. Mitch Hedberg (RIP)
7. George Carlin (RIP)
8. Jerry Seinfeld (multiple times)
9. Jim Gaffigan
10. Lewis Black

"Those hotel rooms are $300 or $400!" said Walt. We were standing in the kitchen, one of the rare occasions I was at his place.

"So what? You can afford it," I said, my arms folded over my chest. "So, I'm not worth $300 or $400?"

"I'm saying, that's a lot of money for a hotel room when we can drive back here and sleep here for free." He was calm, rational as always.

"But that's not what I want to do," I said, frustrated. "I thought we could make a weekend of it. Or at least a night. We still haven't gone anywhere for more than a year." I shook my head and sat down in one of his kitchen chairs.

"I'm not spending $300 on a hotel room."

"Yeah, I get it." I shook my head, deflated. "I hear your 'no' loud and clear." I drained my water glass. I hadn't realized how intractable he'd be on the hotel, but now I wasn't surprised. I shook my head. "This goes beyond the hotel room. You said no to *Hamilton*! To *Hamilton*! Which is probably the most amazing piece of art I'm ever going to experience in my life," I continued. "All of that came out of one person's head: the lyrics, the history, the choreography, and the music. All of it. It was amazing! You had to be there to experience it, and you said, 'no.'"

"You keep bringing that up," said Walt. "That's in the past."

"And the past informs the future." I shook my head, frustrated. "I still want to have adventures, and you don't. When I asked you about retirement, you said you have no idea what you'll be doing. What I was really asking was, do you see me there? What does your life look like?"

"You think about the future," Walt said. "I don't do that. I think about the weekend."

"I have to think about the future," I said. "I have to plan. I have kids. I have to have some sense of what I'm doing, what I'm working toward, and what I'm looking forward to. That's what keeps me going! Otherwise, it's just one more day after day after day."

He was satisfied with so little: his small, simple life, morning news, Judge Judy reruns, hamburgers or brats or pasta for dinner, and golf on Saturday mornings. That was what he wanted.

I wanted more. I always wanted more—more connection, more laughter, and more experiences. More everything. I kept waiting for the universe to work things out for me, when the fact was that I was settling for someone who didn't want me as much as I wanted him and who didn't want anything as much as I wanted everything. What was I doing?

"You know ... I think that maybe we've gone as far as we're going to go," I said, slowly. "You don't want to get married. I don't want to get married. So, what are we doing?" I started to cry. "I think ... I think we should agree to stop seeing each other."

Walt sat there. "If that's what you want."

Again, I wasn't surprised, but it still hurt. I continued to cry, and we talked for a while without saying anything. Eventually, we went to bed. He had to get up early for work, and I was exhausted. He put his arms around me in the dark. "I do love you," he said softly, his breath against my neck.

"I know you do," I said. And it's not enough, I didn't add.

I cried saying goodbye to him the next morning when he left work, and I drove home. When I got home, I sat on my bed and wept in a way I hadn't since my dad died. My heart ached. I was already questioning my decision to walk away from someone I loved, from someone who loved me. I tried not to think of never seeing his smile again, feeling his solid warmth against me in bed, or his reaching over in the truck and rubbing my fingers with his thumb, his skin rough against mine.

I talked it through with Hannelore and Jill and tried to build my resolve. I made it through the next days, sad and exhausted, barely managing to meet my deadlines at work. I offered my Gaffigan tickets to my friend, Maureen, who stopped by to get them.

"But Walt's such a good dude!" she'd said, concerned. "I don't think this is really over between you guys." That was Maureen, who'd been part of a happy couple with her husband since they met in college. Naturally, she wanted the same kind of destiny for me, but Walt wasn't Glenn. He wasn't going to go all John Cusack on me and hold up a boombox blasting Peter Gabriel outside my house to get my attention. He wasn't going to drop to one knee and propose with a ring. If he did, I would say no.

Still, I grieved. I'm doing the right thing, I reminded myself when I wanted to call him at night. I'm brave, I reminded myself when I had a pit in my stomach seeing the Sunday paper on the driveway and realizing we wouldn't do the crossword together. "I can do hard things," I said when I missed waking up to his usual "good morning" texts. I reminded myself when I wanted to text him.

I talked to Molly a few days later. "I love him. He loves me. He's a good man," I said, starting to cry. "And it's not enough."

"You want a life partner," Molly said. "He is a good man, but he isn't your life partner."

When the kids came home from Erik's four days later, I broke the news as gently as I could. I told them that we loved each other but weren't going to see each other anymore.

"Most important, this has nothing to do with you," I said. "I'm hopeful that we can be friends, eventually, so we'll have to see what happens."

"Whaaaaat?" said Haley, her little face confused. "He's not going to come over here anymore?"

"No, I don't think so," I said. "At least, not right now." We talked for a while, with me trying to explain the idea of still wanting adventures while Walt did not to kids who had no idea what life was going to toss their way.

"Let me say … he said 'no' to Hamilton," I said. Geez! Poor Walt! This might be on his tombstone.

"He said no to Hamilton? Bruh!" Ryan was shocked. "Who says no to super-expensive tickets to Hamilton?"

"Well, he's not into history or musicals …"

Ryan interrupted me. "It's Hamilton, Mom! Who says no to that?"

I almost texted him afterward to let him know that I'd told the kids and that they seemed to be okay, but I resisted. The next day, though, he texted me, asking if I'd said anything to them. I wound up calling him (so much for me doing all of the hard things), and we talked.

He told me that he'd felt like I'd been using him, that he'd been used by other women for money and for sex, and that my pushing for the hotel room had reminded me of that. "How would I know that? You never talk about the women you were with before me." He hadn't. He didn't even talk much about his ex-wife, who had died three years prior. Not like me, who had overshared details about my marriage and the handful of other significant men who had made an impact on me—all in the name of transparency.

We talked, and I admitted how sad I was. "I feel terrible," I said. "But there's nothing for it."

"What do you mean?"

"There's nothing for it," I repeated. "There's nothing I can do. It can't be fixed. It's not like you're going to make a grand romantic gesture." I kept coming back to the same talking points: that we were a mismatch, that I wanted more while he wanted less, and that if we didn't have a future, we should call it now and move on.

And yet, his voice in my ear, that deep, slow, direct voice, both comforted and crushed me. "I don't know what a grand romantic gesture is, but I'll tell you, on our second date, you told me about your kids. I knew that someone I dated would probably have kids but thought they'd be older. Like in college. I knew your kids were younger, and that was okay with me." He paused. "They're great kids." He paused again. "I love them. I love your kids. I miss them, and I miss you."

My heart squeezed hard. "I know you love them. They love you, too."

"I've thought about you this whole time, about how much fun we've had. You've been the best girlfriend I've ever had, probably."

"Probably?" I teased. "You shouldn't say probably."

"Okay, for sure. Number one, you've been the most fun girlfriend I've ever had," he said. "Number two, the most sexual."

"I thought you didn't care about that."

"I do. You are. And I just know that when I'm laying down and you're in my arms, I'm the happiest I've ever been. I'm so happy and calm and I fall asleep in five minutes."

"You fall asleep in five minutes anyway," I reminded him, ignoring his grammar, but I felt it, too. The comfort of his arms around me and his warmth against my body made me feel sheltered. Protected. Loved. "I know," I admitted. "But we have to get out of bed sometime."

"I also didn't think I'd ever fall in love again," he said. "But I did." Again, I felt the same. Discovering that I could love a man again—a good man, who was sweet to me and made me laugh—and have that love returned had been a gift I hadn't expected. I was grateful for it even as I realized I needed to let him go even if it hurt.

What was I left with? My own resilience. It could have been so much worse. I could have been where I was four years before: in an outdated, dilapidated, filthy house with not enough work and too many bills; reeling from the divorce, trying to figure out how to handle it and make sure my kids were secure, loved, and, please, God, not totally fucked up as a result; doubting that I would ever have sex again, much less want to have sex or even want someone enough to kiss him again; grieving the loss of my marriage, my stability, my expectations, and the biggest of all, the idea of raising my kids in a loving, supportive, two-parent environment; and oh, yeah, how was I going to work hard enough and make enough money to support myself and them and still pay the bills ...

Well, shit.

I'd come through that, hadn't I? Without Walt. Without any man. I could do this, too.

The Corporate Newbie's Cheat Sheet: How to Manage Your Time More Efficiently

Be honest: how good are you at managing your time? If you are good at it, that's great. If you struggle, however, that lack of skill will likely impede your productivity at work.

Here are my five go-to strategies for time management that are worth adopting:

1. Know your personal productivity cycles. I'm a morning person by nature, so I tackle my most challenging tasks first thing. If your brain doesn't start humming until mid-morning, use that time for yours.

2. Make lists. At work, I keep a running to-do list of all of my projects. As clients' keywords were approved

for outlines, I added them onto my work list and did the same with writing assignments and other projects that had "hard" deadlines." Yes, I still sometimes feel overwhelmed when I look at my work list, but I'm less likely to forget a deadline or client when it's made it onto there.

3. Ignore your email. Seriously. Research shows that it takes several minutes to get back into what you're working on after a distraction. Don't open it every time it chimes; if you must, check it every couple of hours.

4. Reboot, often. I take a break every hour, even if it's only to get up and get more tea, go pee, walk the hallway for a minute or two, or to let myself read Dlisted.

5. At the end of your workday, review your work list and schedule for tomorrow, and make your list of priorities. Then, leave work at work. Your brain will reboot by the next morning, but you help it do so by leaving your work at the office.

CHAPTER 11

Conversion

Back in the office, I found myself frequently staring into space, unable to concentrate on simple tasks. There is no way through but through, I reminded myself. You are brave. You can do it. I had stretches where I didn't think of him at all, but then sadness would swirl in around the edges of my thoughts. I took deep breaths, read Dlisted, and reminded myself that emotions are temporary.

In the meantime, I needed that raise. I asked to meet with Frank on Wednesday morning to talk about what I should and shouldn't say in terms of proving my value. He'd told me he had little wiggle room regarding raises once the partners had determined the budget for different positions and different departments for the year. That was the issue. I didn't want to be treated as a position—as a content specialist. I wanted to be treated as Kelly, a unicorn who brought all kinds of value to the company, thanks to my work.

"You're the most assertive person we've had in this company for a long time," Frank said. A piece of me took umbrage at his word choice. If I were a man, would I be considered assertive? Nope. A go-getter, I supposed.

"But you're coming into this with a freelance mentality," Frank said. "I think you've always been used to having to look out for yourself. I realize that, but you need to be able to put some trust in someone else to make your case for you."

He meant himself, I realized, and I wanted to be able to do that. At the same time, it was impossible to undo 20+ years of being solely responsible for my own success or failure. "If I don't carry my own flag, who's going to do it for me?" I said. We talked for a bit, and I decided to leave nothing unsaid.

"I like working here. I like the company, I like what I'm doing, and I like the people I work with," I said. "I want to stay here, but I have to be making more money. I deserve to make more money. I don't want to leave, but I also don't want to have to keep freelancing," I said. I was still freelancing for several reasons: to keep my hand in, yes; because I wanted to retain my reporting and writing skills; and because I liked the satisfaction of crafting a piece I knew was good for clients who appreciated me. Mostly, though, I was freelancing for the money. I needed the extra income to make my life, and the kids' lives, go.

"I want to feel that the partners value me, for me," I said. "And that they're paying for my experience, not just my time." I knew how productive I was at work, and after nearly a year, I was figuring out the right pace: enough not only to get what I needed done but also to feel like I'd accomplished something at the end of the day—yet not so much that I was spent or bitter at day's end. That was a new challenge I hadn't expected about the work world. My mindset/efficiency/connections framework didn't address it, though I had gleaned a few insights.

"You know, the key to success in the corporate world comes down to one thing: learn how to make your boss happy," I said. "Nothing else matters."

"Well, that's a starting point," Frank agreed. I told him that I'd write up a formal request for a raise, similar to the one I'd submitted in the summer, and I agreed to let him carry my flag. The idea still chafed, but Frank was truly the only person who knew not only what I did all day but also how valuable that was. I'd learned that circumventing him wasn't the answer. Maybe trusting him was. I squashed down my inner freelancer. She hadn't been all that helpful in my corporate adventure. A freelancer might not put faith in anyone but herself, but an employee would put faith in her boss.

That night, I swung by the store to buy chili ingredients. The company was having a chili cook-off and a pumpkin carving contest the next day. While my knife skills were lacking, I had a recipe for chili that I'd been making for years. I cooked a double batch and invited Erik over for dinner. The four of us ate, and afterward we played Old Maid. After he left, I worked on Nancy's final book edits for a while. It was a full, productive day.

The next morning, however, I was left with sad emptiness, the pit in my stomach, the ache in my chest. My whole body ached. I forced myself to run on the treadmill, banging out two-one intervals for four miles. That eased my usual morning anxiety, but sadness swelled in to fill the void. Still, I stuck it out and didn't text or call Walt. I was relieved that he didn't contact me, either.

A few nights later, I'd dropped the kids at Erik's and was getting ready for pool when I heard a knock on the door. Walt was standing on the back door stoop in his work clothes. He looked stricken, tired, and dirty.

"I just thought I'd get my stuff," he said. "I'm sorry I didn't call."

"It's okay." We hadn't talked about when he'd get the clothes he kept at my house: sweats and casual stuff along with his sport coat, dress shirts, and slacks. I opened the door. "Come in." I was so rattled to see him, I couldn't even look at him. When I did, I could see he was angry.

"I gotta say, I don't think you're all that grown up," he said. "You broke up with me without even trying to talk about it."

"We have talked," I said. "I don't know what else there is to say."

My heart hurt to see him in so much pain. I sat down on the bed. "I'm willing to listen."

He talked. I listened. He pointed out that I'd rarely come to his house and that when I was there, I didn't stay that long. True. That he had almost always come to me. True. That we had done a lot of things I wanted to do while rarely doing things that he wanted. Also true. I realized, belatedly, how selfish I'd been. I hadn't realized how one-sided our relationship was. I'd only been focused on what I was, or wasn't, getting from him.

I took a deep breath and patted the bed. "Sit down if you want," I said. "I'm not going anywhere."

He gestured at his work clothes. "I'm all dirty."

"You know I don't care about that."

He sat down on the other side of the bed, and I felt his anger dissipating. "Lie down," I said, stretching out next to him. I felt his body relax next to mine, and he put his arms around me. I felt that sense of comfort, of rightness.

We lay there for a minute. "I miss you," he said. Holding me tighter.

"I miss you, too," I said. "But it feels like I'm always wanting more from you than you can give me. I can't stand the imbalance." I pulled his shirt loose from his pants and slid my hand over his stomach. He radiated heat, as always. "But I'm sorry. I'm sorry for how selfish I've been." I sighed. "I'm sorry for everything."

"I'm sorry, too," he said. "You know I love you."

"I love you too," I admitted. I lay there for a minute, considering. I didn't want him to leave, but I couldn't miss pool. I sat up and looked at him. "Do you want to spend the night?" I knew he was working in Palatine, which was at least a half-hour from my house but more than twice that from his.

"You serious?"

I nodded. "I just can't miss pool."

"Yeah. I'd like that. If you want to."

"Take off your clothes. I'll throw them in the wash. Get in the shower. I'll warm up the chili. Then we can eat, and I'll go to pool." We ate dinner at the kitchen table, I went and played first for my pool team and was home by 9:00 to find him in bed, watching TV. I pulled on my pajamas and got in bed next to him.

"Hey," I tucked my body against him without thinking.

He put his arms around me. "This is when I feel the best," he said softly. "I'm so happy when I have you in my arms."

"Me, too." We lay there talking for a while, and he tightened his grip on the side of my hip, stroking me gently with his thumb.

"I love this part of you, your hips," he said against my ear. "I love to see the curve of your body when I'm behind you like this." My body responded to his touch, like always. I arched my back against him, kissed him again, and then pulled away.

He looked at me, a question in his eyes, and then kissed me. I stroked the side of his face, relaxing in his arms, and pulled him on top of me without saying anything. He stopped before he started to slide inside me, his weight on his forearms. "I love you," he said, leaning down to kiss me gently. He'd never said that to me during sex, only in response if I said it first.

"I love you, too." I pulled him against me, and he moved in me, slow and sweet and steady, waiting for me. After I orgasmed, he kissed me again before he started thrusting in me harder. I could feel the weight of his body, his warmth, his maleness. After he came, he rested his head on my shoulder and then kissed me again.

When I came back from the bathroom, I curled back into his arms. "I love you, and my body loves you, too," I said. It was true. Why deny it?

I expected him to fall asleep immediately, like he usually did, but he pulled me against him, hard. "I'm so scared of losing you," he whispered against my neck, smoothing my hair with his hand. "You think I didn't notice when that guy was watching you at Q," he said. "I saw him. I was watching him."

I'd forgotten about that. A few months before, Walt and I had been practicing at the table nearest the bar. I was dressed for work, with a dress and heels on—business-like, not sexy. We'd been playing for a bit when I became aware of a guy checking me out. He was turned all the way around on his barstool, openly staring and making no effort to hide it. Maybe nothing else was capturing his attention, not even the large screen TVs blasting six different sports simultaneously, but I was getting creeped out, especially when I had to bend over the table to shoot. I tried to ignore him and eyed Walt, wishing he would say or do something, but he was oblivious.

After a good ten minutes, the bouncer, a beefy guy in his 30s, walked over to me from across the pool hall and gestured at the guy with his head.

"This guy bothering you?"

He had noticed the creepy dude from across the bar, and my own boyfriend, standing a few feet away, hadn't?

"No, it's fine," I said. But it wasn't. I'd felt uncomfortable, though not nearly as uncomfortable as if I'd been alone. What would I have done then? Either ignored him as best as I could, or maybe said hello or nodded to him so that he knew I was aware of his attention, striking a balance between not-too-friendly (because I didn't want to engage with him) and not-too-unfriendly (because, as a woman, I was always aware that he might get aggressive, nasty, call me a bitch, or otherwise make me even more uncomfortable). This was part of being a woman and being in the world.

"I've been in a lot of fights, and I'm not going to start one. But if he would have said or done anything to you, I would have taken care of it," Walt said now. He shifted so he could see my face. "I wouldn't let anything happen to you. I'm always paying attention. I would take a bullet for you. I mean it. I couldn't stand it if something happened to you or the kids," he'd said, startling me with the emotion in his voice.

"Hopefully, it won't come to that," I said gently, but I was moved. My former husband, their dad, had never said something like that. No man had.

Even more important, I believed him.

But we couldn't stay entwined in bed forever. He left for work in the morning without our having resolved anything. At the office, I was exhausted and manic. I talked a little trash to the whole office about my chili ("kid- and teen-tested and approved—even my ex-husband loves it!"), babbled on to Melissa, telling her random stories I'd probably shared before, and tried to sell the sales guys on my chili for more votes. I was starting to feel like I belonged at work, slowly gaining traction with fellow employees outside my department. I still thought the place was weird and disconnected, but maybe every workplace is.

I had an appointment with Molly that afternoon, one of the rare occasions that therapy coincided with my immediate need for therapy. I brought her up to speed on the last few weeks and told her what had happened the night before. "He talked to me in a way he never has before," I said. "We had a really good conversation." It had been mostly him talking, though, with me listening. That alone made it unusual.

"What made it so good?"

I thought for a moment. "It felt like... he was open with me," I said. "Vulnerable." Walt had never seemed comfortable with big emotions. I thought of how he'd told me he was scared of losing me and of how hard that must have been for him. "But I've felt so out of balance with him."

"You've regressed," she said. "When you met Walt, you were confident, independent, and taking care of yourself. Now you've slid back into feeling anxious, insecure, and needy."

Ouch! She was right. The needier I'd become, the more I'd driven him away. He'd become my personal lightning rod. When I felt anxious, I blamed him for not making me feel secure. When I was bored, I blamed him for not being exciting enough. When I was worried about what my future looked like, I blamed him for not talking about a future together to give me something to hang on to.

Yet, he'd shown up at my house, not just the night before, but nearly every weekend to see me, almost always bringing something he thought I might need. Cat litter. A new storm door. A toilet for my basement bathroom. A dish rack to replace the battered one on my kitchen counter. A skateboard for Haley because she'd said she wanted one. He'd met me at Ryan's out-of-town basketball tournaments and watched him play. He'd cooked burgers for us, quizzed Haley on her times tables, played endless hands of Old Maid, and fixed everything in my house that needed fixing. He'd shown up for me, not with Peter Gabriel blasting from a boom box, but in his own methodical, thoughtful, measured way, while I blamed him for not being edgy or exciting enough.

I asked Walt if he'd consider seeing Molly with me and had been surprised when he'd agreed. "If you think it will help, I'll go. Just tell me when."

At work the next week, I participated in a client call with an AM and a client who wasn't happy with the content we'd produced for her; all eight landing pages needed to be revised. I listened to her feedback and made notes to pass on to Frank. She was eager to get the new content loaded onto the site right away. "Is there any way you can get the pages done by the end of the month?" she'd asked.

It was the 28th of the month already, and I knew I wasn't allowed to promise any deadlines. "We can try," I said. "I can't make any promises, but we can try."

I passed along my notes to Frank and wasn't surprised when he asked me to revise the pages ASAP. I had to deliver four pages within two days and four more two days after that, which pushed the deadline into the next month. I wanted to beat that and give the client what she wanted. If I pushed, I could do it. I finished four pages the morning of the next day and started researching the next four that afternoon.

The client offered short-term personal loans, and we were to create new landing pages for the different states in which it operated. The client had complained that the pages we'd written were too general, and on review, I'd agreed. Why not take a more personalized approach by appealing to the residents of each state instead? I put on a metaphorical reporter's hat and did some background research for the relevant pages, coming up with a different approach for each page.

For Missouri, a state of primarily solo commuters, I pointed out how a major car repair could upset your finances. For Wisconsin, I mentioned that one in five people visited the emergency room every year (ignoring the question of what the hell are people doing in Wisconsin?) and that unexpected medical bills could upend your budget. For Idaho, the lower-than-average per capita income might mean that you had no emergency fund.

This wasn't a simple optimization task or even the typical writing task I had where I used existing content to create a new page. I called this "Frankensteining," where I grabbed content from a client's website, rewrote it so it wasn't identical to existing content, and cobbled it together to meet word count. Instead, this was a full-on writing assignment, where I had to research, learn, then make decisions about how to approach the page, keeping the client's parameters in mind, and then write it. This was what I loved about freelancing—immersing myself in a subject, doing background research, interviewing experts, and then creating a piece of writing that hadn't existed before.

I finished the last four pages the next day, and Sarah edited them that afternoon so that the AM could forward them to the client. Bam! Challenge met. All eight pages, delivered by the end of the month. Frank sent a note to both of us, thanking us for turning them around so quickly. I felt a satisfaction that was relatively rare at work—of being able to dive deeper than I usually did, to use all of the parts of my freelance brain instead of trying to cram keywords into recalcitrant copy or using unnecessarily convoluted phrases to hit word count.

Before the quarterly meeting the next day, Matt stopped me in the hallway. "You know, we were down in Atlanta the last couple of days," he said. "The AMs were just raving about you, about how much of a difference you've made on the client calls, and about your professionalism and what a great job you're doing."

"Wow! Thank you, Matt! I really appreciate hearing that." I was so surprised I got a little choked up. Geez, don't cry at work, I reminded myself.

"Just passing it along." He smiled and walked into the meeting. That was promising for my raise, right?

The next afternoon, Walt came with me to my session with Molly. It was strange to have him there, and I felt protective of him, afraid that Molly might say something that would hurt him. I sat on the couch where I always did, while he sat in a chair in his work clothes, looking out of place and yet comfortable as always.

"Why did you bring Walt here today?" Molly said.

I glanced at him. "I love him. I know he loves me. I … want to see if there is a way that we can work through this," I said. "I don't want to simply walk away from him without—without trying."

Molly turned to Walt. "What about you?"

Walt cleared his throat. "She asked me to," he said, nodding at me. "I know it's important to her." We talked for a few more minutes, and then Molly surprised me again.

"Kelly needs to feel special," Molly said to Walt. "She loves you, but she craves excitement and adventure. When you tell her that you're thinking about going somewhere for the weekend, that you want to take her to a new restaurant, or that you're working a side job so you can do something with her, that makes her feel good."

I started to interrupt. Molly was making me sound so juvenile, so needy. Then, I closed my mouth. I did need to feel special. Appreciated. Loved. I was still working off my marriage the same way a dieter worked off a long junk-food-laden weekend of carbs and crap. That was what I needed to work on with Molly next—how I could move past needing to feel special and simply be happy and satisfied being me.

A few minutes later, Molly turned to me. "And you have to let Walt be Walt."

But that wasn't all. I needed to stop expecting him, and our relationship, to set the stage for my life. I had thought for so long that a relationship was the framework, the foundation from which I could pursue what I wanted. I'd done that with my marriage. Now, I'd started to flip the script. I had to be my own foundation. The strength of that foundation determined not only how happy I was but also how needy I was in any relationship with a man.

Molly had been right when she'd said that Walt wasn't my life partner. No man was. My life partner had been there all along, but I'd overlooked her. It was up to me to decide what I wanted, to create meaning in my life, and to plan my future. Walt couldn't make me happy. He couldn't heal the parts of me that still felt scared, lonely, and anxious sometimes. That was up to me.

At work, I had talked to Seth, the SEO manager, about a keyword issue I'd noticed—that often, all of the keywords included the client's city and state. A client's keywords might be "dermatologist Naperville, IL," "best dermatologist Naperville, IL" "Naperville, IL dermatologist," "dermatology Naperville," "Naperville, IL dermatologist," … and so on. Incorporating all of the keywords proved challenging. After all, you typically only mentioned the location of the client once, maybe twice on a landing page. You certainly wouldn't keep repeating "Naperville, IL" throughout the content.

"It sounds like I have Tourette's," I told Seth. "The content reads like, 'blah, blah, blah, Naperville, IL! Blah, blah, blah. Naperville, IL! It sounds ridiculous."

That was the challenge of writing SEO content. Yes, you needed a certain number of words that Google could crawl on a page that included the relevant keywords along with a strong meta description and primary header tag to help improve your rankings. But you weren't only writing for the algorithm. You were writing for human beings—the human beings who would read the page and hopefully be convinced to purchase your product or service. SEO might drive them to the page, but the quality of the content helped determine whether they would convert.

Seth said he'd had feedback from AMs that clients were pushing back on it, too. Another issue? The keywords were so narrow, using city and state, there was little or no search volume for them, so it was harder to track the progress of clients' campaigns. A few days after we spoke, he announced a new SEO policy; now the client's city and state would only be used in the primary keyword, in the primary header. That made sense. I had nothing to do with the new policy but felt vindicated regardless.

I was working for a big new client, a vein treatment center with locations around the country. It was a large account that would mean a lot of content—20 pages/month of both landing pages and blog posts. Frank had told me that I'd be writing most of the content for the client and to make that content my first priority. "If that means you leave Melissa with the outlines, so be it," he'd said.

The assignments started rolling in. Many were for blog posts. What is a deep vein thrombosis, or DVT? Is there are a connection between varicose veins and heart disease? Can athletes get blood clots? Why do my veins look blue or green? How many veins are in the human body? Can standing cause varicose veins? I was back in my favorite groove, writing service-oriented health pieces. I wasn't interviewing primary sources the way I would for a freelance piece, but I could do the background research and then distill it down into compelling content, inserting the relevant keywords as I went.

With this much work on my plate, I could work ahead a bit. If I had a piece on varicose veins and heart disease due on Wednesday, I'd start the background research for it on Monday, write a draft on Tuesday, and then finish and proof it on Wednesday. In the meantime, I'd start researching other pieces. I liked working like this. It let me jump between different tasks—researching, distilling, writing, editing—during my day and work with my natural rhythms.

I always used the mornings to write, which are the heaviest lifting I had to do, and prioritized my tasks for the day. That didn't mean that crises couldn't arise that might not have to be addressed ASAP but eliminating the ugliest—tackling the task I most didn't want to—had always worked for me as freelancer, and it worked for me now, too.

One morning in mid-November, Frank asked to meet with me in Yahoo. "I already talked to Melissa about this on Friday; we're going to be hiring a new content specialist and a new editor for the content department," he said. "I've spoken with Sean about your request for a raise, and you're going to get a title change."

I nodded.

"Also, Sean and I went over your request and the work that you're doing, and I think the partners see your value," said Frank. "I'm more a believe-it-when-I-see-it kind of person, but I think you'll be happy with what the partners are going to do for you."

Did that mean I was getting my raise? At least $55,000? "I will?"

He nodded.

"Can you tell me now, or do I have to wait until my review?"

"You have to wait," he said. "But I thought you'd appreciate it knowing it now."

"It's all I can do not to jump up and shimmy," I said. "But I'll restrain myself."

"We're hiring another content specialist to help Melissa. Doing outlines isn't your strength." He corrected himself. "I mean, you can do them, but there are other things you're doing that are a better match for your skills." He listed the types of work I'd been doing. "You've been on the kickoff calls. You've been on client calls and have often done the revisions. You've created model pages for other writers with some of our biggest clients. You've come up with blog topics for Sean and the CMS department, and you're my lead writer, not by volume, but by ability."

Wow! That was the nicest compliment he'd ever given me. "Thank you. I really appreciate it." The ability to craft something that was readable, thoughtful, and well-organized (and yes, incorporated the appropriate keywords) mattered to me. It's what had let me succeed as a freelancer for 22 years, and even if it wasn't always required for my current job, the fact that I still had it—and that he recognized it—mattered.

I didn't want to go all Sally Field on him, but I was touched and deeply appreciative that he'd shared this with me now instead of making me wait six more weeks.

"Question," I said. "Does Sean think I'm a loose cannon?"

Frank stifled a laugh. "Yeah."

"Is there anything I can do to manage him better? I remember you telling me that he said I had asked a lot of questions. I got the impression that that annoyed him, but I always ask questions. I want to know how things work and fit together. I like to understand things."

Frank thought a minute. "Yes, but Digital Edge hasn't hired anyone like you before," he said. "Your personality isn't the typical personality here. Most of the people who work here are more robotic and do their work and the only questions they might have are directly related to what they're doing."

"Robotic? Really? Have you already been reading my diary?" I laughed. "But I see what you're saying."

"It's not that Digital Edge is wrong and you're right or that you're right and Digital Edge is wrong," said Frank. "It's just a place where you don't really fit."

Yes! Yes! That was it. I didn't really fit—except that I was starting to fit and starting to like it. It might not give me the community I was seeking, but who was to say that another company would? I had Sarah. And Melissa. I liked the sales guys and the SEO guys, and I was getting to know the AMs. I loved working from home three days a week.

"It's not like Sean has ever said that you're not getting the job done," he added. "Or that you're a pain in the ass."

Before I could say anything, he smiled. "I'm not saying that I haven't said that …"

I burst out laughing. "Yeah, I knew that was coming. Guilty as charged." But the mood in the room was relaxed. I was a pain in his ass sometimes, and I was okay with that. I could see that despite our earlier conflicts, Frank and I could work together. I did respect him even if I didn't agree with some of the decisions he made, and while I got tired of trying to tiptoe around his ego and territoriality, he could have been more difficult. He had given me much more freedom than he had to.

After our conversation, I called Melissa in for a meeting and shared the highlights of the conversation. I asked her about her future, and she was in a holding pattern, at least for now. Why shouldn't she be? She was in the first year of her first real job. Why ask what she wanted? She might not have any idea yet. Although we worked together, I didn't know her that well. I knew she liked hockey and had a way more engaging

Instagram presence than I did (then again, didn't everyone else on Instagram?), that she lived with her parents, and that she apparently thought I was funny (at least I hoped so), but work relationships by nature aren't necessarily deep. Maybe she liked me. Maybe she didn't. Maybe she just thought I was this crazy old woman she was forced to work with, which I pretty much was.

"You know, you've done the right thing since you started here," I said. "You've kept your head down, worked, and haven't made any waves." That's what I should have done, I realized, and said so. "I've made some mistakes," I said. "And now I'm thinking … maybe I want to see how far I can go here. I don't want Frank's job … I'm not good at all of those spreadsheets and tracking individual pieces of content, but maybe I do want some kind of managerial role." I shrugged.

Shit, I likely had already ruined my chances at that, given my oversharing, constant questioning, loud laughing, and occasional swearing. Then again, that was the person I was, wasn't it? I might not be manager material. I could see that conversation happening eventually, but for now, if the company was willing to give me what I wanted, at least what I wanted now, I was willing to stay.

In the following weeks, I followed my own advice to Melissa. I kept my head down and worked. I set goals for each morning, whether I was at home or at the office, and checked them off as I went along. At home, Ryan was settling into his role of moody teenager who spent most of his time at home on the Xbox and answered me in monosyllabic grunts while Haley was her usual bouncy, chatty self. The dog had given up on eating the furniture in favor of a steady stream of chew toys, though she still liked to sit on the ottoman by the living room window and bark explosively at anyone who walked by.

The cat remained her queenly, arrogant self, draping herself across my lap and laptop when the spirit moved her.

Walt had been working jobs near my house more often, spending more nights there. The four of us would eat dinner together and hang out for a while before the kids peeled off to the siren songs of their screens. Walt had run out of items to fix or replace at my house, but I knew he'd come up with some eventually. It was how he showed me he loved me. In bed, he'd wrap his arms around me and pull me against him, and I'd fall asleep. When I had to switch sides, I'd tap his shoulder and he'd roll over, still half-asleep, and I'd tuck in behind him, my arm wrapped around his belly. That vague feeling of not-quite-right had disappeared. Now I was left in the quiet. In the calm. In the space that I so rarely found.

Short List of Items Walt Repaired/Replaced/Updated in My Home (Without Me Ever Asking)

1. Replaced bathroom toilet with a new one
2. Replaced storm doors to my front and back doors
3. Rewired electrical outlet in the living room and added an outlet cover
4. Replaced the dryer vent with a new one
5. Replaced old laundry tub with a new one twice the size of the old one
6. Replaced my bedroom light fixture with a new one that included a fan
7. Fixed my bathtub drain
8. Fixed the storm door to the sunroom
9. Rehung a new American flag and added a bracket for the flag
10. Hung LED lights in Haley's bedroom, and when Ryan decided he wanted them, Ryan's room as well

Walt had surprised me earlier that month. I was sitting on the couch, scrolling through ticket prices for *Hamilton*. The show was closing, and I'd decided to take the kids a second time. "I know, you think I'm nuts," I said, as he looked over my shoulder. "But we all want to see it again."

He got up a few minutes later, returning with a credit card he tossed in my lap.

"What's this?" I said, holding up the card.

He nodded at my computer screen. "Buy four tickets."

It took me a minute. "Are you serious? You don't have to go."

"No, I want to go." He grinned. "But only because I never want to hear 'you said no to *Hamilton*' ever again." I'd laughed and booked the tickets.

Molly had told me in our most recent session that I'd done a lot of hard work. "You have to know that you can handle anything," she'd explained. "Not just know it logically but know it in your gut." Walking away from Walt, even though I loved him, had proven that to me. I had been heartsick at losing him. I had also been okay. I hadn't fallen apart or been unable to work or take care of my kids or even take care of myself. I was stronger than I'd realized.

When he'd shown up for me, I'd had to decide whether I would be backsliding to stay together. I'd realized I needed to ask more from myself and less from him; to stop blaming him for I thought he lacked when the issue was always with my own insecurity and neediness; and to realize that a relationship, no matter how good, wasn't the answer.

What was? Loving myself. Loving my kids. Loving my friends and my family. The fact that I had a brain and body that worked, pretty well at least most of the time, and being grateful for that. Loving an unexpected moment of connection with a stranger or laughing with Hannelore or Jill or Polly, an endorphin-producing run, cuddling in bed with Haley in the morning while we critiqued the fashion of The Weather Channel meteorologists, taking Ryan golfing and watching him drive the ball farther than I did, or simply sitting around the kitchen table playing Rummikub or Old Maid with the kids after dinner. I still missed the freedom of my freelance life but realized there was freedom in structure and predictability as well.

A few days later, Frank asked me into Yahoo. He sat down and folded his arms over his chest, his usual position. "I met with Sean this morning, and he told me the salaries for my staff," he said with little preamble. "You're getting a salary increase of $10,000."

It took me a minute. At first, I thought he'd said 10 percent. But he'd said $10,000. I wouldn't have minded more, but I was getting my raise. I could make that work.

"Really? Thank you. Thank you!" I almost hugged Frank, but I restrained myself. "That means a lot. It means that the partners value me and want to keep me ... wow. I really appreciate it. Thanks again." We talked for a couple of minutes, and I walked back to my desk, humming under my breath. I quickly ran numbers. It was a 22.22 percent raise! But it wasn't just the money. It was the "yes." We appreciate you. We value you. We want you.

I emailed Frank that morning to formally thank him for presenting my case to Sean and the partners. I told him I knew that I wasn't the easiest employee to manage and that I appreciated his faith in me. I had taken a chance on the job, but he had taken a chance on me.

What had I learned in the past year? That work wasn't nearly as satisfying as freelancing, and yet the former had taught me a lot. I had learned about SEO, Google, keywords, backlinks, PPC campaigns, decks, spreadsheets, and SOWs.

I'd learned to work with people again. I'd learned to bend to a boss and had been able to do it without breaking even if my heart still beat with a subversive rhythm. The freelancer in me still lived, but I could keep her happy with occasional assignments for clients I liked working for. Doing so stretched my writing muscle in a way that my job did not, and that alone made freelancing worthwhile—even if now I wouldn't absolutely need the money.

Frank had asked me more than a year before why I would want this job. Now I realized I hadn't wanted the job itself or even the health insurance. I'd wanted security, or at least the illusion of it.

Now that I had that security, at least for the moment, what did I want?

To continue to say yes instead of no, to stay open to new possibilities even while I embraced what I was lucky to have, to accept my flaws and goofiness and ambition and ego and tendency to overshare and anxiety and everything else that made me, me.

To thrive no matter where I was planted, whether that meant freelancing, working, or a blend of both.

To love the people I was lucky enough to have in my life.

And to trust—not only in the universe, but in myself as well.

The Corporate Newbie's Cheat Sheet: Getting Better at Being Grateful

I wrote quite a bit about gratitude as a freelancer, but I'll distill it down: gratitude is good for you. Expressing gratitude produces a cascade of positive emotional and physical health benefits, including boosting immune function, improving your sleep, enhancing your overall outlook, and helping you feel more connected to others.

Yet, often we forget to be grateful and instead focus on what we lack instead of what we have, like that you're making less money than you'd like instead of appreciating that you have a job—hopefully a job that you can tolerate, if not downright love. Yeah, sometimes, work sucks. Sometimes, life does. One of the easiest ways to change your mindset it to think about what you're grateful for instead of what you're unhappy about.

Do you like the people you work with? Do you enjoy what you're doing? Do you have an easy commute, a boss who appreciates you, or (wait for it) decent health insurance? Remind yourself of the pros of your job, not just the factors you'd like to change, and you'll feel better about your career.

And why stop there? When I'm down, overwhelmed, or simply cranky, I list some of the many things I'm grateful for. A strong, resilient body. Healthy kids. Friends who make me laugh. Some money saved for retirement. The ability to pivot, adapt, and thrive, no matter what challenges I face.

When you do the same, you'll find that you can almost always shift your mindset, and your outlook, for the better, regardless of what you're facing. Give it a try, and I think you'll find that it works.

About
Kelly K. James

Kelly K. James (formerly Kelly James-Enger) has been writing for a living—whether as a freelancer, fulltime employee, or both—for more than 26 years. She is the author of thousands of articles and more than a dozen books, including *"Writer for Hire: 101 Secrets to Freelance Success"; "Six-Figure Freelancing: The Writer's Guide to Making More Money, Second Edition;" and "Goodbye Byline, Hello Big Bucks: Make Money Ghostwriting Books, Articles, Blogs, and More, Second Edition."*

Kelly lives, runs, writes, plays 8-ball, and attempts to golf in the Chicago suburbs. She shares her home with two awesome teenagers, a rescue pup, and a very fat spoiled cat. You can reach her at kellykjames@kellykjames.net, through LinkedIn at Kelly K. James, or on Instagram at @healthbookghost.

9 781957 354361